FREESTYLE

FREESTYLE

TIM STREET-PORTER

The New Architecture and Interior Design from Los Angeles

With an Introduction by Pilar Viladas and an Afterword by Paul Goldberger

Stewart, Tabori & Chang
New York

The author and publisher gratefully acknowledge the
support of *House & Garden*, and their permission to
reprint the following photographs, all by Tim Street-Porter:
pp. 63, 199 © Condé Nast Publications Inc., *House &
Garden* September 1980; pp. 70 (left, bottom right), 96, 97,
98, 99, 198, 200, 201 (both) © Condé Nast Publications Inc.,
House & Garden February 1982; pp. 110 (bottom left), 111,
113 (both), 115 © Condé Nast Publications Inc., *House &
Garden* February 1984; pp. 219, 220, 221 (both) © Condé
Nast Publications Inc., *House & Garden* March 1985;
pp. 152, 155 (bottom right), 157, 161 (both), 208 (both), 209
(both), 212–213, 214 (both) © Condé Nast Publications Inc.,
House & Garden April 1986.

Published by Stewart, Tabori & Chang, Inc.
740 Broadway, New York, New York 10003

Library of Congress Cataloging-in-Publication Data

Street-Porter, Tim.
   Freestyle, the new architecture and design from Los
Angeles.

   Includes index.
   1. Architecture, Domestic – California – Los Angeles.
2. Los Angeles (Calif.) – Buildings, structures, etc.
I. Title.
NA7238.L6S77   1986   728′.09794′94   86-5812
ISBN 0-941434-91-5

Distributed by Workman Publishing
1 West 39 Street, New York, New York 10018

Printed in Japan

CONTENTS

PART ONE

THE HERITAGE

Los Angeles is a city of contradictions. The ubiquitous silver light can bleach everything it touches into pale perfection as readily as it can outline in an almost cruelly sharp focus. On a clear day you can take in sun-washed beaches and snow-capped mountains in a single, panoramic sweep. Palm trees grow side by side with pines. The intoxicating fragrance of jasmine and orange blossom on a warm evening can obliterate the memory of the acrid smog blanket that had smothered at noon. Steep-sided canyons are prey to dry-season fires and rainy-season mudslides, yet people continue to line them with houses that perch perilously on stilts. Weeks of benign weather can suddenly give way to blistering Santa Ana winds or torrential rains.

Sprawled at the edge of the vast Pacific, Los Angeles is twentieth-century America's frontier. A city created by means of irrigation and railroads, it was founded by pioneers and continues to attract them. Brashly American in its optimism, materialism, and dependence on the automobile, Los Angeles is also keenly aware of its Spanish-colonial origins and its relative proximity to the Far East, both of which are reflected in its diverse mix of resident ethnic groups. The sun-bleached landscape and the combination of sensuous luxury and disquieting seediness have figured prominently in the works of such writers as Nathanael West, Raymond Chandler and Joan Didion, as well as those of artist Ed Ruscha, with his enigmatic "word" paintings, and David Hockney's swimming pools and palm trees which have acquired an almost iconic status in the imagery of Southern California. Seen by millions as a place of promise and unlimited possibilities—"California, Here I Come"—Los Angeles became the city where fantasy and reality were often indistinguishable; an image fueled by the city's relative youth and by its two major industries, film and aerospace, each providing its own gold mine of fantasy, whether via space flight or merely a flight of fancy.

It is hardly surprising, then, that Los Angeles came to be known for its fantasy architecture, its man-made environment having burgeoned during this century. A genre that flourished during the 1930s and 1940s, producing such memorable structures as the "witch's house" in Beverly Hills, the Danish "village" apartment court or the drive-up doughnut stand topped by—what else?—a giant doughnut, its culmination in the 1950s was an entire kingdom of fantasy architecture—Disneyland.

(Even today, fantasy houses continue to appear: the O'Neill house in Beverly Hills is an extravagant, minutely detailed homage to Art Nouveau.) But well before these exercises in kitsch became identified with the laissez-faire atmosphere of the stereotypical Lotusland, the modern architectural pioneers of the United States and Europe were discovering that the same culture that, without even blinking, accepted a building shaped like a boat, would also tolerate, even encourage, serious architectural innovation. The perception of perpetual new beginnings and infinite possibilities that drew pioneers to the area a hundred years ago has continued to attract architects whose ideas and experiments might have been discouraged elsewhere. Unencumbered by long-standing traditions or prejudices, successive generations of twentieth-century architects have left their mark in Los Angeles, creating what may be the richest diversity of residential architecture in the United States and making the city a laboratory for design invention.

Experiments in residential architecture began in Los Angeles early in the century. Charles Sumner Greene and his brother, Henry Mather Greene, helped to create a new genre of American domestic architecture, often called the California Bungalow, with a number of houses (the Gamble House among them) in nearby Pasadena. A hybrid of the bungalow type of wooden house (developed for the hot and humid climate of India) and the American Shingle and Stick styles of the late-nineteenth century, Greene and Greene's highly personal style produced houses with low, overhanging pitched roofs which shaded wide porches designed for sitting and sleeping, reflecting the era's concern for "healthful living" and prefiguring modern architecture's attempts to bring the outdoors indoors. Inside, the houses are masterpieces of craftsmanship, blending both Arts and Crafts and Japanese sensibilities in their simple but exquisitely joined woodwork and Tiffany-glass windows and light fixtures. While other architects helped the California Bungalow style proliferate throughout the state, it was Greene and Greene who gave the style its highest expression and, in their sensitive response to the time and place, the Pasadena houses comprise an important chapter in the history of American domestic architecture.

While the Greene brothers were building their eclectic wood houses, Irving Gill was even more directly paving the way for modern architecture. His buildings skillfully incorporated the forms of Spanish Colonial adobe architecture—low arches, courtyards, and loggias—with the rigorously unadorned, cubic masses of the buildings that were beginning to appear in European cities, those that would lead to the International Style architecture we know today.

In the 1920s, while the mania for European-born Art Deco architecture was sweeping the country (including Los Angeles), another wave of pioneers arrived on the West Coast bringing new ideas with them. Having left both a lucrative practice and a large family in Oak Park, Illinois, and having recently returned from a trip to Japan, Frank Lloyd Wright arrived in Los Angeles looking for a change of scenery and, subsequently, the new architectural forms that were appropriate to that scenery. His most famous Los Angeles house, Aline Barnsdall's Hollyhock House, reflects Wright's penchant for the dramatic, blocklike forms of Mayan architecture; its sprawling horizontality speaks of his desire to open it up to the sun and breezes, a luxury he never had in the more extreme climate of the Midwest. It was also in Los Angeles that Wright conducted his first experiments in textile-block construction, a system of precast concrete blocks "woven" together with steel rods, that Wright believed would enable the building of well-designed houses at moderate prices. While only a limited success, the experiment produced four residences—the Millard, Storer, Ennis and Freeman houses—in and around Los Angeles. Their dramatic forms, which incorporated influences from Japanese and Mayan architecture with Wright's own Prairie School style of the early 1900s, made these houses at once solid sheltering masses, and cool airy pavilions, situated to take advantage of daylight and breezes. At the same time, Wright's son, Lloyd, set up a practice in Los Angeles, designing houses even more dramatic than his father's, like the Sowden House in Hollywood.

It was also in the 1920s that Viennese architects R. M. Schindler and Richard Neutra arrived in Los Angeles and began to build houses as radical as Wright's, both in their interpretations of European Modernist principles and in the unprecedented manner by which they blurred the lines between inside and outside, as in Schindler's Lovell Beach House, or Neutra's Health House (also built for the Lovells). Using such simple materials as concrete, wood, stucco and ready-made steel windows, Schindler and Neutra developed a style of architecture that

The tropical surroundings of this 1920s Hollywood house belie its Normandy style.

consisted of interlocking volumes, transparent corners, and an emphasis on the horizontal—all of which were pioneered by Wright in his Prairie Houses. This style went on to become identified with Southern California and to pave the way for experiments such as the Case Study program of the 1940s and 1950s.

In the years during and after World War II, the booming defense and aerospace industries were responsible for the birth of new technologies which, in turn, influenced the architecture of the era. New materials and building methods were employed to satisfy the soaring postwar demand for inexpensive, well-designed housing. The Case Study program, organized by *Arts & Architecture* magazine's editor, John O. Entenza, brought together a group of masters of the Modern style including Neutra, J. R. Davidson, Rafael Soriano, Pierre Koenig, Craig Ellwood and Charles Eames, to design houses which responded to such realities of contemporary life as smaller families, fewer servants, and skyrocketing land values. These houses, generally small and simply laid out for easy maintenance, were built of lightweight materials with large areas of glass. While such houses could not be built today—California energy codes restrict the amount of glass used in new buildings—the Case Study houses made an important contribution to the architecture of the period, and to the history of domestic architecture in America. They became as closely identified with Southern California as had the bungalows of half a century before. While their influence was not as pervasive in the mass housing market as was that of another California architect, Cliff May, whose ranch houses were ultimately adapted into one of the most common house types in the country, Entenza and the Case Study architects carried out what was certainly the most cohesive effort to develop new forms of postwar housing.

The postwar era also produced a boom in industrial design and jet-age imagery ranging from the sublime (Charles and Ray Eames's molded plywood furniture) to the ridiculous. Los Angeles still contains many well-preserved (or well-restored) 1950s houses, such as the Erenberg House.

The technological innovations of the 1950s and 1960s gave way to the electronic revolution of the 1970s and 1980s, creating an entirely new set of much less easily defined problems for Los Angeles architects. The pioneer spirit no longer resulted in technological innovation that could be translated into building materials; instead, it produced the microchip and fiber optics. As technology itself was becoming less and less tangible, the revolution in electronic communications—including film, television and video—was producing its own imagery within our culture, affecting not just architecture but the fine arts and graphic design as well. And, just as important, this shift was concurrent with the time in which the architectural profession as a whole was being thrown into a state of upheaval by the widespread rejection of the Modernist principles that had shaped many American cities since the war, creating one steel and glass "box" after another. Even in Los Angeles—which, because of its vast amounts of open space, was relatively late in filling its downtown with skyscrapers—architects were rebelling against the style that produced buildings stripped of ornament, pattern, color and comprehensible scale. In repudiating a philosophy that, by applying the same forms to all buildings, effectively failed to distinguish between houses and office buildings and ultimately between big cities and small towns, architects sought to return to historical precedents for meaning and human scale in buildings. Generally called post-Modernism, the movement that resulted was in part conceived in the landmark writings of architect Robert Venturi and planner Denise Scott Brown, and was given prominence in the United States by the work of their firm, Venturi Rauch and Scott Brown, as well as by the work of Michael Graves and, most important for the West Coast, the work of Charles Moore. Having moved to Los Angeles in the late 1970s to teach at the architecture school at UCLA, Moore designed buildings that offered an eclectic, lighthearted and sensitive blend of regional and historical styles, of fine and "cheap" materials (often side by side), of shifts in scale and distortions in perspective reminiscent of a favorite trick of his seventeenth-century Baroque antecedents. Moore's "inclusivist" approach to both architectural history and the visual world (his own house in Southern California is crammed with Mexican handcrafts and personal artifacts) couldn't be further removed from the rigidly minimalistic approach favored by Modernist architecture and its design of interiors and furniture, and his work exemplifies the marked shift in architectural theory that has taken place in the last decade.

This climate of eclecticism has produced a similar flowering of new forms among the younger generation of Los Angeles architects. Eugene Kupper's house for singer Harry Nilsson, and multiunit housing projects such as Urban Forms's Sun Tech houses, a condominium development in Santa Monica that incorporates a rather European approach to planning, with its units in villagelike clusters, and demonstrating a modern concern for both active and passive solar design features, are only two examples. The shapes, rhythms and materials of the surrounding urban landscape are freely mixed with quotations from past American and European styles in an effort to make people feel more at home with the built environment, to appeal to our collective memory and sense of historical continuity and to add texture and richness to our everyday lives. (P. V.)

13

The Hugo Reid Adobe in the Baldwin Rancho, Santa Anita (1839). This simple structure with thick adobe walls faces a raked-dirt courtyard with a well.

A 1930s Zig-Zag Moderne house in the Wilshire District.

The Rancho, built by entrepreneur "Lucky" Baldwin, also includes this lakeside Victorian folly, now the L.A. Arboretum.

Even the miniature-golf courses around L.A. have their own fantasy architecture.

The Osiris Apartments (1926). Although it fronts the more usual stucco box, J. M. Close's monumental pylon façade speaks of the Egyptian-Revival style popular during the 1920s.

Above left: *Villa d'Este Apartments (1928). Its sequence of seductive courtyards and tiny fountains places this among L.A.'s collection of exceptional apartment complexes in the Classical style.*

16

*The lobby of the 1920s Amen-Ra Apartments in East Hollywood continues the Egyptian-Revival theme of its exterior.
Prompted by the discovery of King Tut's tomb in 1922, this revival led to the construction of at least twenty
Neo-Egyptian apartment buildings, many of which still exist.*

Opposite: *O'Neill Residence, Beverly Hills (1981).
Designed by Don Ramos—the plaster carving executed by
Stephen Hart—this residence was built to house the
owner's collection of art nouveau furniture.*

18

Hightower Court, Hollywood Hills. Featured in Raymond Chandler novels and movies, this canyonside community is accessible from the street below via a 1930s elevator tower, or by a narrow pathway and steps. Reminiscent of Mediterranean hill towns, an early Lloyd Wright house can be found nestled among its trees (right).

Opposite: *The Sun-Tech housing by Urban Forms, Santa Monica (1981). A villagelike cluster of condominiums incorporates active and passive solar design facilities; their stepped grid motifs derive from 1970s New Wave graphics (top). A single line of very expensive houses occupies this precarious strip of Malibu Beach (bottom).*

Danish Village Apartments, Beverly Boulevard (1925). Built by a Danish immigrant to remind him of home, this "village" courtyard is enclosed both by apartments and a large studio for its artist creator.

Opposite: *Spadena House, Beverly Hills (1921). Henry Oliver's quintessential "witch's house" was originally built as a movie set for a production company in Culver City, and later was moved to its present location.*

The low-budget fantasy of this 1920s Moorish-style apartment building in Silverlake is limited to its front façade—behind the arch lies a conventional courtyard.

They resemble drive-in dinner trays clipped to the side of a mountain, but these houses are for the intrepid only. This mode of building, with its inherent great views, became popular in the 1950s (top). The saucers have landed—one anyway. John Lautner's Chemosphere House (1960) hovers in the Hollywood Hills (bottom).

Opposite: *Sowden House, East Hollywood (1926). Known locally as the "Jaws House," this is Lloyd Wright's most exotic design. It is built around an inner courtyard which today is dominated by a giant cactus.*

Overleaf: *Nestling below a rocky outcrop, this 1970s house, and its locale, are reminiscent of early TV Westerns. Constructed of adobe brick, it houses owner Snuff Garrett's unique collection of Western memorabilia.*

Gamble House, Pasadena (1908). The California tradition of indoor-outdoor living finds an early expression in this masterpiece built by Greene & Greene for the Gamble family (of Procter & Gamble). It has been fully restored, down to its original furniture and fittings.

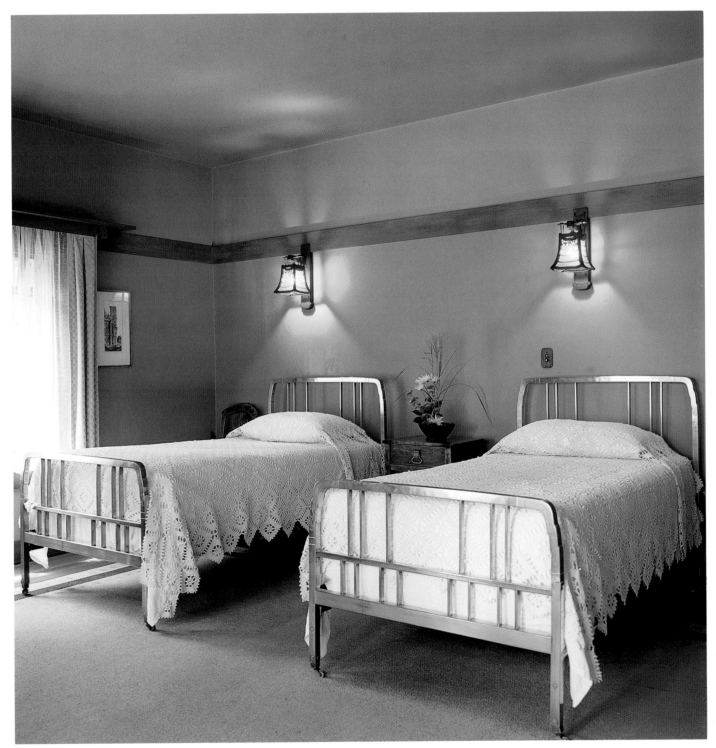

The beds in this guest bedroom were designed by the Greene brothers, who had them finished in nickel silver which was then engraved with a wild rose pattern. The Tiffany-glass lamps, designed by Charles Greene, also incorporate this wild rose motif.

The focal point of the dining room is this large table, its Honduras mahogany matching the wood elsewhere in the room and the Tiffany chandelier having been designed to complement it.

The tile of the dining room fireplace is studded with Tiffany-glass inserts. Above it, the cabinets feature Tiffany Favrile glass.

Opposite: *The master bedroom embodies several master touches, including this black walnut writing desk and chair. The desk's handcarved panels are inlaid with semiprecious stones; the floor lamp is by Tiffany.*

This Tiffany-glass lamp hangs from leather straps over an inglenook in the sitting room. Its Burma teak is hand-finished with smooth rounded edges.

Opposite: *The Burma teak woodwork of the entry hall is finished, as elsewhere in the house, with rounded corners, giving it an exquisite smoothness to the touch. All wood joints are pegged—no nails or screws were allowed—and these pegs are important elements of the visual expression. The lamp on the side table is by Charles Greene.*

Storer House, Hollywood Hills (1923). The justly famous house by Frank Lloyd Wright has been lovingly restored by its current owner, film producer Joel Silver, whose renovation team—led by the architect's grandson, Eric Lloyd Wright—has transformed it from near ruin to its original "showroom condition."

Opposite: *Light from the French doors filters into the sitting area through a perforated concrete-block balustrade. The couch is a Wright design, but built under the directions of the present design team.*

35

The Lloyd Wright table and chairs from the 1920s add a touch of Cecil B. DeMille to the second-floor living area.

36

The master bedroom. Of special note is the chair by Carlo Mollino from the 1950s. The bed, vintage 1930, is from the owner's previous home.

Opposite: *A chair built to a Wright design for the design team. At right is a glazed sliding screen which opens to allow air to enter through a perforated exterior wall.*

Howe House, Silverlake (1925). Rudolph Schindler used frameless glazing to dramatize the indoor-outdoor relationship of this house. Above the living room is a sleeping platform. Immediately outside the window is a light well which is protected by the soffit overhead, and illuminates the floor below.

Lovell Beach House, Balboa Peninsula (1922–1926). This Schindler house is composed of a complex series of structural and decorative elements. The double-height living room has a gallery down one side, which gives access to a row of bedrooms. De Stijl decorative elements relieve the extended wall surfaces.

Opposite: *Articulating the space below, the twin entry stairs of the Lovell Beach House rise up through the concrete frames which support the living areas overhead.*

Mandalay (1953). Occupying the head of a pretty valley surrounded by wild hillsides, Mandalay is the home of its creator, architect Cliff May, who was the pioneer of the "ranch-style" house. The versatility of this style can be seen here by the way later additions have extended the original design to include courtyards and a large dovecot.

Opposite: *The skylit entry lobby, seen here from the large living area, has an entire wall of bookshelves filled with vellum-bound volumes from May's travels. Rooted in large planters, indoor plants have grown to the size of small trees.*

Originally an outdoor patio, the dining area is now enclosed. The deeply recessed window frames a view of meadows beyond. The dining table is from the William Randolph Hearst estate; the chairs are from Spain.

Opposite: *This Mandalay fireplace was also designed by May. The ranch-style origins of the house have been modified over the years to reflect the architect's love of traditional Mexican architecture. The original timber column has been replaced by one of stone.*

Eames House and Studio, Santa Monica (1947–1949). Built as part of the Case Study House Program, the original High-Tech house looks as contemporary today as when Charles and Rae Eames first built it.

44

The dining room of the Fuller House (see opposite) enjoys a view of the city—as though in Cinerama.

Erenberg Residence, Mar Vista. A Chrysler Dual Ghia, that most chic of 1950s cars, is an apt complement to the exterior of this well-restored house on a suburban tract of the same vintage.

Alan and Lori Erenberg have restored their living room to fully live up to its 1950s potential. The reupholstered couch is a tour-de-force of freeform design.

This 1939 Hollywood Hills residence by Leland Fuller is a fine example of Streamlined Moderne. On a hilltop high above the city, its balconies resemble the promenade decks of a vintage ocean liner.

The Erenberg dining room is lined with wallpaper designed for the Beverly Hills Hotel. The table is a 1950s imitation of a Noguchi original.

A study opens onto the Erenberg's backyard. The unusual floor lamp features a swiveling disc that acts as a reflector for the lamp itself, which is set into the base.

The starburst chandelier, vinyl-covered banquette, Formica-and-chrome dinette and speckled linoleum floor all contribute to the Erenberg kitchen's feeling of being right out of a 1950s Saturday Evening Post *advertisement.*

Opposite: *The painting by English artist Duggie Fields dominates the living room.*

Above and opposite: *Allee Willis Residence, Studio City (1937). Built as a party house for MGM, William Kessling designed this elegant Streamlined Moderne structure. Today it has the very latest in desert landscaping—cactus and bowling balls set in sand and trimmed with glass brick—created by Willis.*

50

Studio residence, Hollywood Hills (1979). This simple studio house by Steven Ehrlich is used for painting and photography. The stairs lead to a second-floor bedroom.

Seen here from the bedroom balcony, the glazed corner makes the most of an attractive north-facing canyon view. 1920s tropical furniture and a handpainted canvas rug by Annie Kelly complement the architecture.

Opposite: *Nilsson Residence, Bel Air (1977). Built for singer-composer Harry Nilsson, this handsome house is integrated into its canyon environment with careful terracing and landscaping. Architect Eugene Kupper produced a house of complexity, a gabled, navelike space running its length. Classical and Mediterranean forms provide suggestions of post-Modernism, but with a pleasing restraint.*

Above, left and opposite: *Yudell/Beebe Residence, Ocean Park (1984). A tiny 1920s vacation cottage transformed by architect Buzz Yudell and his wife, color consultant Tina Beebe. Using windows salvaged from a nearby cottage facing demolition, they modified the façade while maintaining the character of the original. Originally six rooms, the interior now consists of a single space plus a bathroom. To increase the apparent space, Yudell devised an interior ellipse whose line is defined by columns, overhead beams, and even the curve of the banquette. The various parts of the house which occur outside this ellipse lend to the illusion of greater depth.*

The bedroom of the Rodes House is tiny, with storage below the bed. The shelves and window provide close-at-hand amenities to compensate for the snug dimensions.

Rodes House, Brentwood (1979). A plant trellis is built-in to each end of a convex neo-Classical façade. The house is fronted by a herb garden planted by its owner; beyond is an orange grove and a view of the city.

For the owner, who is a professor of English at UCLA, architects Moore, Ruble & Yudell maximized the living space to enable him to stage theatrical productions. A lighting grid to which extra lights and gels can be clipped spans the concave façade wall and continues outside as the plant trellis.

PART TWO

THE NEW WAVE

While the tenets of post-Modernism—drawing heavily on European architectural history, and formulated largely in the academic atmosphere of East Coast schools— were (for better or worse) gaining widespread acceptance, a number of Los Angeles architects and designers were conducting their own, quite different, architectural experiments. Rather than alluding to historic architectures of the U.S. or Europe, they preferred to mine their own backyard: the architectural heritage of Los Angeles which, though hardly more than a century old, is rich with source material. The new buildings and interiors of such architects and designers as Frank Gehry, Morphosis, Eric Owen Moss, Frederick Fisher and Brian Murphy refer as much to the physical culture of Los Angeles—its exotic landscape, freeways, light—as they do to local architectural traditions. (Since such traditions are relatively new, these architects draw largely on a Modernist, rather than a classical, tradition, which may be why they seem, for the most part, to find post-Modernism an alien concept.) The architects also draw inspiration from both the building process and materials themselves. Therefore, the new L.A. houses tend to consist of rather abstract, unadorned forms, in such "banal" materials as concrete and galvanized metal, stucco, asphalt shingles and plywood.

With the exception of Gehry's work, many of these new experiments have been for residential and small-scale commercial projects. Their work frequently considered too radical to appeal to real estate developers, many of the architects work alone or in very small firms. But, however small some of the projects may be, their influence on the architectural profession, in Los Angeles and far beyond, has been considerable; Los Angeles in the 1980s is regarded as the source of some of the most inventive architecture in the country.

If this "new wave" of architecture can be said to have started anywhere, it was with the Gehry House in Santa Monica. Frank Gehry, the senior, and most controversial, member of the group, shocked the architectural profession when he transformed a modest Dutch Colonial house on a quiet suburban street into a three-dimensional Constructivist collage that seems to defy the laws of gravity and certainly defied the conventions for contemporary buildings. Gehry, who had spent a decade working for large commercial firms before founding Frank O. Gehry & Associates in 1962, had been a fairly orthodox Modernist until the 1970s when he realized that the commonly held distinctions between "pretty" and "ugly" were no longer relevant in the architectural, economic and social blender that the United States—especially its cities—had become. It occurred to him that buildings look better under construction, that "unfinished" is better than "finished." Consequently, Gehry began to find his sources in the "anonymous" forms of the low-rise structures that made up the Los Angeles streetscape, along with the basic, no-frills materials they were made of—concrete block, sheet metal and chain-link fencing, to name a few. Gehry now maintains that the "cheapskate" materials that became his signature were less a matter of preference than of necessity: they were inexpensive and didn't require skilled labor to assemble. Nonetheless, they became an integral part of the vocabulary of the Los Angeles architects who were influenced by him. Gehry was also the first architect in many years to take an active interest in contemporary art, noting the influence that sculptors such as Carl Andre, Donald Judd, Larry Bell, Richard Serra and Claes Oldenburg have had on his own work. This is especially apparent in their uncompromising, minimal forms, and their use of "tough" materials that transform the commonplace into the extraordinary.

The asphalt floor of the kitchen addition in the Gehry House is a reminder of the old driveway which it replaces. A new cabinet wraps around the original bay window.

When seen in the context of his other buildings, Gehry's own house is actually an anomaly. It seems much more an abstract sculptural composition than architecture that addresses the issue of its urban or suburban context, a trait that characterizes much of his subsequent work. Gehry has increasingly tried to break up the monolithic forms of large buildings by turning them into a series of smaller forms which seem more at home among their low-scaled neighbors. For example, the Indiana Avenue houses, built as artists' studios, comprise a group of three two-story volumes packed into a narrow lot in a rundown section of Venice. While a single large building would have looked out of place on the lot, Gehry's irregularly shaped forms, clad in utilitarian asphalt shingles, plywood or stucco, neither imitate the forms of the tiny bungalows and "dingbats" (L.A. shorthand for its ubiquitous cheap stucco boxes) that line the street, nor do they fight them.

Less than a mile away, near the Venice Beach boardwalk (a no less dilapidated, but more expensive, part of town), Gehry's Spiller House stands out somewhat from its neighboring single-family and small apartment-house buildings. On the outside it is a tough-looking volume clad in corrugated galvanized steel; inside, however, it is a light-filled treehouse of exposed wood beams and stairs. The construction is intentionally rather crude; the house was meant to be built on a small budget, so Gehry allowed for construction that did not include costly detailing or high levels of finish. But the space and light are what count in this soaring interior, and Gehry is a master at incorporating both. In spite of the generous amounts of daylight and views, the house's decks are carefully camouflaged from public view, an important factor in a community often mobbed by beachgoers.

Directly on the boardwalk is one of Gehry's more recent and most colorful houses, designed for screenwriter Bill Norton and his artist wife, Lynn. It is an exuberant, eye-catching combination of stepped, boxlike forms, with a swimming-pool-blue tiled base, pipe-railed terraces and a "lifeguard tower" study that perches out over the second-floor terrace. As outrageous as the house might seem on its own, in the context of its boardwalk neighbors—older houses decorated in what might be described as Late Beachcomber style—the Norton House blends right in. Inside, the clean and uncluttered, but narrow, volumes of the house are punctuated

Opposite: *A new skylight over the kitchen area of Gehry's Nelson House allows light to descend through an assortment of sandblasted 1920s redwood beams.*

by numerous skylights and windows offering a constant reminder of the outdoors and admitting light to the house, which is crowded on either side by its neighbors.

Frank Gehry's influence has grown considerably over the past few years, affecting not just the residential landscape of the city but also that of the commercial, civic and institutional sectors, with projects such as the Temporary Contemporary (Museum of Contemporary Art), the California Aerospace Museum, Santa Monica Place and Loyola Law School. He is now receiving major commissions in other cities as well. While his idiosyncratic style and single-minded devotion to his own principles are not in themselves qualities unique to Los Angeles, his ideas have certainly found a more tolerant atmosphere there than would have been the case in

For his Caplin House, architect Fred Fisher created a roof form which resembles a giant wave about to break amidst the palm trees and rooftops of Venice.

many other American cities. Gehry's work perpetuates the Los Angeles "pioneer" traditions of independence of thought and the search for expression particularly suited to time and place. The beauty of this work is that it reveals, time and time again, the seemingly unremarkable to be, in fact, quite remarkable.

Thom Mayne and Michael Rotondi of the firm Morphosis often work with the inexpensive materials and exposed structure found in Gehry's buildings but, unlike Gehry, they take an almost obsessive interest in the careful articulation and crafting of the components of their buildings. While they have designed several commercial projects, they are best known for their residential work, their three Venice "alley houses" in particular.

Many urban residential areas in Los Angeles have an alley system which functions as a secondary street network and which is just as interesting visually as the primary network, crammed with tiny garages and other outbuildings. Small garage apartments or studios have long been indigenous to this alley system, but Morphosis significantly transformed this particular building type with their 2–4–6–8, Sedlak and Venice III house additions. In each of these little buildings, the architects have related the scale and texture of their exteriors to the often ragtag forms and materials of the alley, while providing a visual connection to the expansive views and natural light of the city beyond, for the occupants within. Among the smallest works of contemporary Los Angeles architecture, they are also some of the most memorable.

On the other hand, Mayne and Rotondi's Lawrence House was conceived in a different vein. Rather than being an addition, it is a complete house; instead of consisting of a series of articulated parts, its interior spaces seem to have been carved or sculpted. The house occupies a narrow ocean-view lot in Hermosa Beach, and its uncompromising galvanized-metal façade gives no hint of the complex series of spaces and circulation paths behind it.

Eric Owen Moss, a contemporary of Mayne and Rotondi, shares their interest in articulating the parts of a building for their own sake (very much a Modernist notion). His work is, however, more significant for its deliberate commentary on American domestic architecture—its forms as well as the sociological factors that shaped them. Moss's own 708 House in Pacific Palisades is, like the Gehry House, a startling transformation of a modest, unassuming 1950s Modern suburban dwelling.

The Sedlak House—the second of three Venice alley houses by Morphosis—is detailed to blend contextually with its neighbors and displays the added flourish of New Wave graphics.

Moss's expansion of the house preserves much of the original structure while it exaggerates the new elements—a huge, phony "buttress," a two-dimensional "peaked" roof, the supergraphic street number on the side of the house—thereby offering a satirical view of the kind of house that most residents of suburbia take for granted. By turning these preconceptions upside-down, Moss questions their validity at the same time as he acknowledges their firmly established place in our architectural and social cultures. These ideas are more fully developed in the next house Moss designed, the Petal House in Rancho Park.

Working this time with a slightly more traditional-looking tract house, Moss gave a three-dimensional voice to many of the forms used in the 708 House: the flattened "toy" buttress becomes a "real" solid-timber structural element; the peaked roof really does open up, in petallike fashion, to reveal a jacuzzi and views of the Santa Monica Freeway and the towers of Century City. Much has been made of the freeway in the cultural imagery of Los Angeles, but the Petal House actually incorporates the freeway into the experience of living in the house with surprisingly rewarding results. Its interiors are comfortable, modestly scaled, and sunny and, perhaps more important, the Petal House looks less caricatured than the 708 House; more believable. Driving along the Santa Monica Freeway, the sight of the peaked roof opening above the trees is startling, but not implausible. It is simply speculation come true.

Fred Fisher's work is more difficult to define or categorize. In the collagelike composition, exposed interior structure, distorted perspectives, and use of materials such as chain link of his Caplin House in Venice, the influences of Gehry (in whose office Fisher once worked) can be seen clearly. The Jorgenson House, however, seems to grow out of an entirely different vision, its architectural-ruin imagery stemming from its precipitous site high in the Hollywood Hills. Fisher's attitude toward materials in this house is almost decorative, with paired galvanized-metal culverts forming columns and glazed concrete block and ceramic tile arranged in multicolored patterns. The house's architectural pedigree seems to be more Classical Roman than L.A. Contemporary, yet its forms and materials illustrate the sort of pragmatic and eclectic borrowing that characterizes Fisher's work.

Graphic design has been an integral part of the changing art and design scenes in Los Angeles. The jagged edges of "rip and tear," the mismatched patterns,

A view of Moss's 1982 Petal House from the elevated Santa Monica Freeway.

2-4-6-8 House, Venice (1979). Morphosis settled this exquisitely detailed pyramid-shaped timber roof over the interior space. The blue panel covering the window is an electrically operated air vent.

Satirizing the house's location in a quiet neighborhood, Moss displayed the street number—708—in bold supergraphics. Adding to the humor is the blue-polka-dotted reverse side of the fake roof gable.

In the living room of this 1983 Santa Monica residence, Brian Murphy has included a cluster of bright storage cabinets, shelves, and a sconce, all echoing graphic motifs found elsewhere in the house. Through the tiled archway is the Deco sitting room.

Furniture has also found an enthusiastic audience in Los Angeles artists and architects. Artists such as Peter Shire, Phil Garner and David Hertz, and such architects and designers as Frank Gehry, Grinstein/Daniels, Koning/Eizenberg, Brian Murphy, Lisa Lombardi and Michael Tolleson have all designed furniture, reflecting a renewed interest in both the design and craft aspects of the problem. These interiors and furniture designs reflect an even larger interest in the decorative arts, as well as an effort to reunite architecture and the arts after the nearly fifty years of estrangement that resulted from Modernism's insistence on minimal ornament and on the supremacy of architectural form. The more outlandish of these interiors can, in many ways, be seen as the successors to the earlier fantasy houses of Los Angeles. Whether the imagery derives from the Brothers Grimm (as in the Beverly Hills "witch's house"), or from space travel (like John Lautner's Chemosphere House), these fantasies all depend on an essentially naïve belief in the possibility of a perfect world. In the 1980s, naïveté is no longer a hallmark of mass culture. Most Americans are noticeably less innocent than they once were. And today's young artists are more aware than most people of the tremendous overload in visual imagery and information that bombards us every day. Their witty, fanciful work often represents a rejection of the slick emotionless world of the electronic media, in which all facts are presented equally and uncritically. Just as the Arts and Crafts movement in England was a reaction against the mechanization engendered by the Industrial Revolution, perhaps these artists and designers are trying to save the artifacts of our daily lives from being zapped into nonexistence. If this seems to be at odds with the current L.A. architectural outlook, which has a reputation for cutting-edge timeliness, we should remember that even the most radical thinkers in the Southern-California tradition were pragmatists, and that often for every three steps forward, we take one step back. What is so encouraging about the current L.A. scene is that all these forces are operating in close proximity to one another, creating a rich atmosphere of cross fertilization and shared enthusiasms. Just as the brilliant light, flowering plants, and sense of infinite possibilities inspired creative minds early in the century, new generations of Los Angeles artists and architects, native or immigrant, know a pioneer spirit when they see one. *(P. V.)*

Opposite: *This "fifties Western" furniture in metal, found objects, and cowskin was created by artist Kim Milligan for songwriter Allee Willis. The concrete pedestal comes complete with geological fissures lined with shattered windshield glass.*

CHAPTER 1

TWO ADDITIONS

New house design in Los Angeles runs counter to a predominant recent trend in America, one which has been toward a conservative neo-historicism, usually referred to as post-Modernism. This has helped to rejuvenate the spirit of freedom and innovation so prevalent earlier in the century as exemplified by the work of Wright, Neutra, Schindler and Eames.

The freshness and wit of early post-Modern projects by Robert Venturi has not been sustained over twenty years of seemingly endless variations on the same limited theme: the use of façade-applied motifs laboriously quoted from architectural history. Banality has ensued, leading to a visual Muzak as countless happy-faced imitations dot the countryside, from city hall to fast-food restaurant. Emanating from the East Coast, post-Modernism attempted to be a blending with the classical, European-based vernacular of the older communities whose architecture was originally derived from European roots.

Ignoring this prevalent traditionalism, the new free-spirited L.A. architects have pursued a course of innovation, showing little interest in either history or posterity, their concerns seeming closer to those of contemporary artists than to those of traditional architects. References to the Classical past are, after all, a little irrelevant in a city over 8,000 miles from the Acropolis.

Two projects have been particularly influential in terms of attracting widespread media and critical interest. The Gehry House (1978) launched the movement on an unsuspecting public (making Gehry—whose career to that date was well-established, but obscure—instantly famous).

Designed only three years after British

youths began transforming their appearance with shaved or spiky heads, ripped clothing and safety pins penetrating their facial features, the Gehry House introduced the Punk aesthetic to architecture and presented a similar challenge to the status quo. The horror felt by parents as their beloved offspring contorted themselves into symbols of anarchy and outrage was mirrored by the reaction of neighbors in genteel Santa Monica when they witnessed chain link and corrugated metal – symbols of trashy industrial neighborhoods – enveloping the Gehry residence.

If the Gehry Residence is the most outrageous of the new L.A. houses, Eric Moss's Petal House (1982) is the super-cool apotheosis of the many houses and interiors which have followed it and were inspired by its daring. Moss gave Gehry's approach an updated image: startling, graphic, but with a new refinement. Throughout the Petal House, enormous care has been given to detailing, and the unusually high level of craftsmanship is such as one might expect to find in a traditional boatyard. Common, inexpensive building materials are used throughout, but are made to look expensive.

Both of these projects are additions to existing houses which were in themselves inconsequential and mundane, inviting the usual steps toward "neutralizing" them, making their additions be the entire statement. Instead, both architects took the unusual, if not unique, step of retaining the old houses and using them as integral design elements in the new project and thereby bestowing upon them an importance they never had before. This ability to create a viable aesthetic from the commonplace is an affinity which Moss shares with Gehry, but the Petal House moved this aesthetic in a new direction.

Occupying a corner lot, an old pink house is enveloped by an artfully composed collage of chain link, wired glass and corrugated metal.

The Gehry House

Architect Frank Gehry and his wife Berta bought their "dumb little house" (Gehry's words) in 1977. It was the kind of 1930s clapboard house found in any American city. As it was not big enough in its existing form (the family includes two children), an extension was planned to increase the interior space by 40 percent and to add a roof terrace. Gehry had no initial intention of creating a tour de force. As work progressed, however, the project increasingly evolved into a laboratory for the radical ideas then current in his office. And what better guinea pig than the architect's own house?

By the time the house was completed in 1978, it had caused a major stir in the neighborhood. People in this prim area found it difficult to accept that what appeared to be just a construction fence of corrugated metal was, instead, the permanent wall of the new addition. Moreover, the "nice" old house could still be seen, enmeshed within layers of chain link and glass set at barbaric angles. Petitions of complaint were sent to the mayor (to no effect: she proved to be a Gehry fan and loved the house), and Gehry had to start a petition of his own to a local newspaper in order to restrain its irate urban design critic from directing his dog to relieve itself on the Gehry front lawn each morning. To help defuse the situation, Gehry initiated neighborhood tours through the house, helping many neighbors to understand the house – if not exactly to appreciate it.

Meanwhile, the house was attracting attention far beyond Santa Monica. Appearing in *Time, People,* the *New York Times Magazine,* not to mention numerous international design magazines, it became a celebrity, one of the most extensively published houses of all time.

This was not due to any superficial shock value. The winner of the prestigious Honor Award of the American Institute of Architects for 1979, the Gehry House boldly explored a new approach to architecture, bringing with it a new vocabulary of materials and their applications, and a new freedom from conventional design processes.

As mentioned earlier, the outstanding feature of the Gehry House is that the old house, far from being "neutralized," has been elevated in importance; it is now like a "shrine" within the new work, participating in a dialogue with it. By exposing the original structure right down to its bare joists and laths, a common ground is reached with the new carpentry, which has been kept rough and matter-of-fact. Having united the old and the new in this way, portions of moldings, cornices and window frames are retained here and there, providing visual surprise. Sometimes the old wood is left unpainted, elsewhere it is sandblasted. The redwood thus revealed was a cheap and plentiful material in the 1930s, but is a luxury now.

This dialogue exists everywhere between the old and the new, and it begins the moment that the house is entered. No sooner are you inside than you are confronted with another front door: the old one. At this point you have the option to walk through the second front door into the old living room, or to turn right, down some steps to the level of the old driveway, into the new dining area. This room is "outside" the old house, and you can look through the windows that remain: some glazed; some not. To increase the illusion of being outside, the dining and kitchen areas are paved with asphalt—a ghost of the old driveway.

Beyond the "neighborly" picket fence, one glimpses the new kitchen. The skylight resembles an angled cube that seems to have collided with the house.

Overleaf (left): *A breakfast table is situated between the kitchen and a new glazed exterior wall facing the backyard. Above the table is a Charles Arnoldi painted-tree-branch construction* (top). *From this corner of the living room, the kitchen is visible through the original bay window. A new exterior wall is apparent through old studs which were left in place when walls were removed* (bottom).

Opposite: *Light filters into the kitchen through the large old cedar tree beyond the skylight.*

The kitchen is dominated somewhat by the old bay window, perhaps the single most evocative and surreal element of the old house. A new kitchen cabinet wraps around it with glass doors echoing the patterns of glass in the windows above. As a dramatic contrast, the new skylight— a vast tilted cube—bathes the area with light filtered through an old cedar tree, looking from the outside as if it had crashed into the roof.

The old living room, despite its raw look, is surprisingly cozy. Enwrapped by the new extension, thereby placing the outside world at a greater distance, it has become an "inner sanctum."

Upstairs, the new construction includes an open deck adjacent to the bedrooms, providing balcony space. With the ceiling removed from the upstairs rooms the space soars up to the rafters and an open attic space, accessible from the bedroom by ladder. From this area it is possible, on a clear day, to see Catalina Island.

Gehry's interest in materials scorned by other architects is well-represented here. The folded planes of chain-link fencing convey memories of childhood ball parks. Upstairs they provide enclosure and protection to the terrace outside the children's bedrooms. Most dramatic is Gehry's use of what one critic called "structural striptease," by which he has revealed the layers of construction inside the building. Wood studs

Above left: *The old fireplace was left intact, the surrounding wall having been faced in plywood.*

Left: *From the dining room, a pair of piers can be seen holding up the corner of the old house. To the left is the entry area—the new entry door on the left; the old one to the right—guarded by a sculpture.*

(usually invisible, although nearly every house in L.A.–whether Tudor, International Style, Spanish, French Provincial or Scottish Baronial– is constructed of them), are seen for what they are: the bones of the building. Instead of terminating them at window openings, they pass right through the glazed area, sandwiched between two layers of glass.

This exposure of the building's fabric and construction processes is only part of the story; the architect also used this technique to create a variety of effects–layering, opening up space, creating "accidental" and seemingly ingenuous events. These concerns reflect Gehry's correlative relationship to the work of contemporary sculptors such as Donald Judd, Larry Bell and Richard Serra, whose aims in working with such materials as wood, steel, concrete and glass are not to make beautiful objects, but to explore the nature of the materials themselves.

The attention focused on the original structure and its "memories" gives the old house an importance it previously lacked. In Gehry's words: "When we were starting the construction, people came to me and said 'please don't destroy that nice little house, it's a landmark in this neighborhood.' So I tried to preserve the feeling that it still existed, that we hadn't destroyed it, that we had just made it more important."

Above right: *The bathroom cabinet features a window recycled from the old house and glazed with mirror. Its juncture with the wall was deliberately left unfinished, as if it has been violently pushed into place.*

Right: *The master-bedroom ceiling was removed to reveal an attic space and the roof, accessible via an overscaled ladder. To the left is a study/dressing area.*

Architect Eric Moss has given these exterior steps, leading to a guest house over the garage, a nautical look by means of the bright varnished wood and balustrade of white rope.

82

Opposite: A triangular pool fills most of the available space in the compact backyard. The new kitchen extension is to the left, behind the kennel (a nice suburban touch). Vertical metal steps lead to the rooftop jacuzzi.

The Petal House

Also of humble origins, the Petal House was designed by architect Eric Moss and finished in 1982. It is situated in Rancho Park, a quiet, anonymous suburb near Westwood. The owners, Brad and Maritza Cuthbertson, wanted extra space for themselves and a two-year-old son (specifically an enlarged living room and kitchen, a new master bedroom, new guest house and a pool). Like its neighbors, the house was a typical 1940s tract bungalow; like the Gehry House, it was on a street corner and so presented more than one façade to the street. Moss, like Gehry, used the original house as the key element in his new design.

But, while Gehry ate away at the old structure of his house, Moss elected to keep the existing structure just as it was, using it as a point of embarkation for the additions, and even giving it new roles to play. For instance, the original roof eaves were left intact to project into the new kitchen space, where they "shelter" the refrigerator wall, light from fixtures attached to the eaves' undersides spilling over it.

From the street, the Petal House is distinguished from its neighbors by the mass of its new upper floor, which is exaggerated by tiny window openings and upended roof "petals." The entry door is recessed back from the front line of the house, an existing bedroom wing on the left, and a new caged-in porch on the right. It is painted in a white gloss sheen, and curved to correspond with the circular lobby within, above which is a cupola. To the left of the lobby are stairs carpeted in a piano key pattern (acknowledging one of Brad Cuthbertson's major

The upper floor looms over the old structure. Its bulk, exaggerated by the tiny staircase windows, projects out from the side of the house at the left and is whimsically supported by a sloping timber column. The "petals" give the impression that a conventional pyramid roof has burst open.

Opposite: *The entry lobby is a cylindrical space, visually reinforced by its curved entry door and horizontal striping. Beyond are the stairs.*

interests), and a wall of brightly varnished plywood. This serves as a structural shear wall: instead of hiding it, Moss gave it a high-quality lacquer finish and neat boat-builder's detailing.

The kitchen, spare and elegant, has white cabinets with fluted surfaces, at one point wrapped around a tiny window offering a view of the pool outside. The space is bright thanks to a large skylight and clerestory window. The new master bedroom is served by separate His and Her bathrooms, entered from either side of the bed, joined in the middle by a communal shower. These are distinguishable from the street by a row of tiny square windows.

Above the bedroom, what appears to have originally been a simple pyramid roof has been opened up and out to reveal, surprisingly, a large jacuzzi. This concession to an important part of California culture is situated for convenient eye-level viewing of the elevated Santa Monica Freeway, complete with a giant computerized sign that provides traffic information in verse. Each roof "petal" is tilted at a different angle: a vertical one hides the jacuzzi motor, another slopes outward and is ideal for sunbathing. Each one is laced to its companion with one-inch-diameter white rope—a rather witty non sequitur

Above left: *The new front porch is caged in with rebars (more typically used for concrete reinforcement). Called into service here for security, they also exploit an unexpected decorative potential.*

Left: *The stairs are carpeted in a piano-key motif. To the left is a plywood structural shear wall, left exposed but carefully detailed and varnished.*

as the lacing appears to keep the petals from flying apart.

Always, a clear distinction has been maintained between old and new structure. A "transition zone" stratum is formed by a band of structural shear plywood (necessary for earthquake stiffening) punctuated visually with studs, which normally would be hidden on the inside. This stratum is used to separate the new upper floor visually from the original house below (a device also used with the guest house/garage). A fine example of decorative effects coming from intrinsic structural necessities, this is not something simply added on, as with much post-Modernist design.

In his earlier 708 House, Moss satirized suburbia by employing phony gables and the overscaled display of the street number, then adding a fake flying buttress for punctuation. This fondness for the non sequitur is generously indulged in the Petal House as well: the elaborate prop used to hold up the side of the house (which, on closer inspection, holds up only the stairs), the white-rope lacing used for the roof balustrade and the curved front door, to say nothing of the roof petals themselves. These, and other gentle visual jokes, make this house unique.

Above right: *The eaves of the old house protrude into the new kitchen space below a small clerestory. Lights attached to their underside illuminate the refrigerator wall.*

Right: *The collage of tiles decorating this ground-floor shower unit is reminiscent of the tiled wall at the end of the pool (see p. 59).*

The master bedroom features His and Her bathrooms situated behind the bed, a communal shower joining them. The bedside table is the work of Peter Shire.

Opposite: *The living room, with its Annie Kelly painting over the fireplace, enjoys additional illumination from a skylight. Beyond the Peter Shire coffee table is the dining area.*

The kitchen cabinets are interrupted by a tiny window overlooking the swimming pool.

Opposite: *The dining area, delineated by shaped overhead beams, features this table and chairs by Peter Shire.*

Overleaf: *The roof seems to have opened like a flower to reveal a jacuzzi. Between these "petals" are views of the city, the mountains and the nearby elevated freeway. The "laced" white-rope balustrades appear to be keeping it all from flying apart.*

CHAPTER 2

VENICE

Venice has had a checkered history, beginning with the grandiose dreams of land speculator Abbott Kinney, who opened it as a resort in 1905. He modeled Venice on the original as closely as he could. There were canals–including a mile-long Grand Canal–and Italian gondolieri were imported for the opening festivities. An arcaded Venetian-style main street was constructed leading to the boardwalk and its giant pleasure piers and amusement parks. An efficient trolley service linked Venice with the rest of Los Angeles.

The dream fell casualty to oil drilling and decades of dilapidation; all that is left of it today are a few canals and a short stretch of arcade on Windward Avenue and Market Street. In 1958, a brief flurry of activity ensued when Hollywood descended on the Speedway (an alley running parallel to the boardwalk): Orson Welles arrived to film the famous bravura opening sequence of *A Touch of Evil*. This did little to restore Venice's once proud self-image, however, as the location was used to portray the seedy border town of Tijuana, Mexico.

In 1974, a plan to redevelop much of Venice as an extension of the vast, middle-class Marina complex fell through. With no further threat of bulldozers, a real estate boom quickly developed. Many members of the hippie community were magically transformed into real estate speculators, and are now millionaires. Old shacks and seedy apartments sported new coats of paint, and the "ramshackle" became *"bijoux."*

Today, everyone, or so it seems, wants to live near the ocean. Besides the beach itself, the air quality is superior and the climate temperate– facts which apparently justify real estate prices close to those of Beverly Hills for an area in which much still looks raffish and run down.

Among those who live and work in the "new" Venice are many of L.A.'s artists and architects; it has, in fact, long been an art community due to the availability of cheap industrial studio space, proximity to a surfing beach and a Bohemian environment.

Gehry & Associates' office is located right off the boardwalk in what was previously artist Charles Arnoldi's studio. Architect Steven Ehrlich lives and works in Venice, his office located next door to the 72 Market Street restaurant, under an original Abbott Kinney neo-Venetian arcade.

Venice is also home to a growing number of movie people and young professionals attracted both by a community spirit stronger than any other in the city and the healthy beach life. These have proved to be ideal clients for the radical architects in the area.

Social life revolves around bar-restaurants such as 72 Market Street (designed by Morphosis), the West Beach Café and Rebeccas, a new-style Mexican restaurant with architecture by Frank Gehry. In these restaurants one can find a home-away-from-home neighborliness at one end of the bar, and a "café society" social whirl at the other.

The café society is a 1980s social phenomenon reminiscent of the sophisticated night life of the 1930s. Once again we like to get dressed up according to a prevailing but heterogeneous style, to see and be seen. The favored meeting place has become the bar-restaurant, where one can eat or just drink and socialize. In this informal "cocktail party" atmosphere, artists, architects and their potential clients can meet and get to know each other.

Venice is comprised of small-scale residential streets, lined with 1920s bungalows. Behind these, in an alternating rhythm, are narrow service alleys, some still unpaved, lined with garbage

Glimpsed over the rooftops, the tiny, yet eye-catching window of the 2–4–6–8 House makes the simple profile appear larger.

Opposite: *From the alley, an over-the-fence view reveals the entry lobby created by a projection of the window form outward in three dimensions.*

cans, graffiti, garages and extensive power lines. It is in the backyards of these little houses, facing onto the alleys behind, that Morphosis has built a series of small but distinctive houses.

The area within four blocks of the beach is different. Here there are no front or back yards, and alleys predominate. Many of the lots, originally intended for tiny beach cottages, are filled with condominiums which squeeze in as many rooms as zoning will allow. The resulting landscape is one of a Tokyolike intensity, with buildings packed together in a haphazard, untidy conglomeration, and lacking the neat delineation of sidewalk and greenery so typical of Los Angeles. It is in this part of Venice that Gehry's Spiller and Norton houses were built. Immediately behind this area is a multiracial, high-crime community known as the Venice Ghetto, which is itself surrounded by middle class areas that are beginning to make the inevitable inroads into what is in effect the Westside's last cheap real estate.

The Alley Houses

Mike Rotondi and Thom Mayne of Morphosis have built a series of small backyard additions—studios and guest houses—which have been carefully integrated into the dense fabric of alley streets so typical of Venice. The 2–4–6–8 House was the first of these. Designed in 1979 as a cube with a pyramid roof, it combines overall simplicity with a complexity of detail. It is intended as a retreat, a place to study music and practice Zen. The name refers to the relative size of each of its four windows which range from tiny to oversize, and completely alter the apparent size of the building when viewed from different angles.

Set into one side of the simple cube space, the smallest of the four windows is seen here from the inside.

The 2–4–6–8 House is located in the back garden of a 1920s beach cottage and is owned by John Sale, a software designer for IBM. Situated over a garage with views up and down a typical Venice alley—bearing the romantic title, Amoroso Place—it is clad in materials which are quoted from the immediate environment.

An entry porch is neatly incorporated into a projection of the largest of the four apertures. Once inside, the room is lofty and serene, with an exquisitely detailed timber roof, and a quiet gray carpet. The windows, placed high for privacy and to edit out surrounding buildings, provide a view of palms and sky. Designed as complex organisms attached to an otherwise simple box, the windows are controlled by a large, and initially startling, switchplate by the door. They are double-glazed, with metallic louvers set on the outside of the glass and a yellow-painted timber cross superimposed on the exterior frame. The blinds open and close—or retract altogether—at the touch of a switch. Above the windows, in a thoughtful separation of function, blue-colored vent flaps can be opened and closed, also electrically.

Truly a tea house for the 1980s.

Venice III is the third alley project by Morphosis. Finished in 1985, it is the closest to being a complete, self-contained house. Attached to a trim, pretty 1920s bungalow (it was commissioned by Anne Bergren, a classics professor at UCLA), it contains a library/living space, a workroom, bedroom and bath.

Reached via the kitchen, the new library/living area is lit by a lightwell, adjacent to the stair, projecting through from the upper floor and allowing sun from the skylight to penetrate through to the lower level. French doors open onto a small lawn. Below the stairs a small study is set below grade. The bathroom is above this on an intermediate landing, and the airy space of the bedroom provides views over the neighboring roofs toward the Santa Monica Mountains.

The exterior is clad partly in asphalt shingles —the favored contextual material for new Venice architecture. It is organized into three distinct towerlike forms: two rising up through the building and capped by skylights, a third housing the study with bathroom above, and topped by a tiny roof terrace. The skylights are shielded from the sun by canopies, attached by a system of ropes and pulleys, pivotal steel compression members and concrete counterweights. This confection has more to do with sculpture than practicality, however. It works beautifully as the former; its practicality is somewhat tempered by the occasional need for removing and replacing the canopies, a major undertaking that necessitates a call to the architects.

For the remodel of a small Venice beach house on a limited budget, Fred Fisher concentrated on textured surfaces for impact. Ceilings were removed and new skylights added, rendering the space bright even on a foggy day.

The kitchen cabinets were sprayed with Zolatone, a durable industrial spray finish that comes in an infinite variety of colors and variations. This one, a gray fleck, resembles "shelf paper granite" as Fisher calls it. The floor and stairs are 1950s-style vinyl. The flourish was left for the marble-clad fireplace which gives an opulent feel to the entire project.

"8"—the largest of the four windows—combines architecturally with the entry door.

Preceding pages: *The living room/library of Venice III is bathed in light from all sides. Surmounted by a large skylight, the stairs leading up to the bedroom function as a light well. Below them is a small study with a bathroom above. French doors lead out to a small garden on the right.*

Page 101: *Winner of the 1986 AIA Honors Award, the Venice III addition is to the rear of an attractive 1920s bungalow, its striking form topped by white saillike canopies (top). To the right of the large airy bedroom is a balcony. A storage wall behind the bed acts as a room divider (bottom).*

Fred Fisher removed walls and ceiling to reveal this airy space, illuminated by skylights and enlivened with unexpected textural treatments. The coffee table is an onyx remnant crowning a crumpled sheet of lead.

Opposite: *The fireplace, surrounded by a plane of contrasting rose marble and blue granite, acts as the focal point for the room.*

The Indiana Avenue Studios are an imposing addition to the Venice Ghetto, a multiracial neighborhood whose architecture is predominantly of the small-bungalow variety.

Indiana Avenue

The three Indiana Avenue studios, designed for a group of Venice artists by Frank Gehry, were conceived as a real estate venture in 1981. They were constructed as empty shells to enable buyers to add kitchens, bathrooms and finishes according to taste.

Indiana Avenue is in the midst of the Ghetto, and this complex is considerably overscaled for its neighborhood of tiny bungalows. In an effort to compensate for this—conceptually at least—each unit has been given an oversized element to make it look smaller: a Dutch gable, a chimney, a staircase. Each is placed on the façade like a giant brooch, imparting personality to the otherwise blandly imposing units.

Each studio is given a different surface treatment to further stress its individuality. The front one is dressed with green asphalt shingles; the middle one sports unpainted plywood; blue-painted stucco adorns the third.

Above and above left: *The exterior of the front unit is sheathed in asbestos shingles and is further distinguished by its "staircase," attached to the façade like a giant brooch. The interior shows the exposed framing for the other "staircase" on the front façade.*

Left: *The interior of the middle unit, the studio of artist Anne Pixley, who was the first to occupy the building. The space profits from its dramatic windows placed at various levels.*

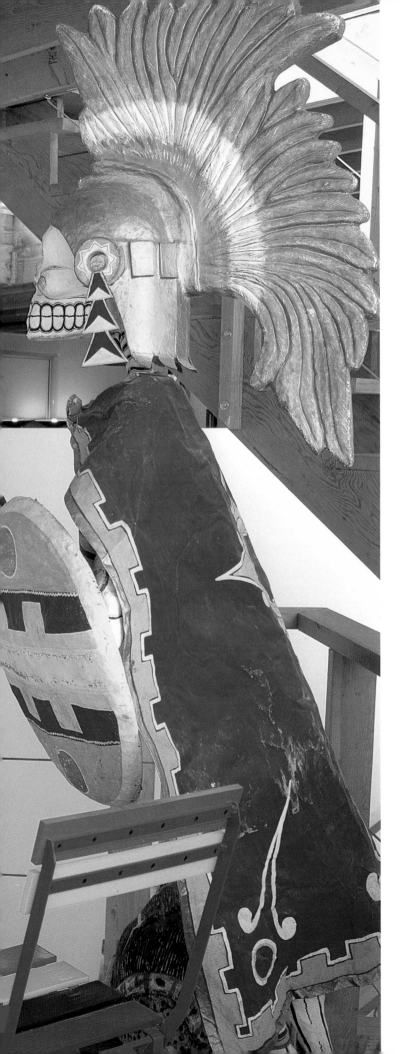

The Hopper Studio

After lying empty for three years, the rear stuccoed unit was bought by actor Dennis Hopper who hired Brian Murphy to convert the empty box into a comfortable apartment. Murphy created within the twenty-foot-high space a second level, reached by a simply detailed timber stair, deliberately echoing a vernacular established by Gehry elsewhere in the complex. The bedroom, to the left of the stair, is placed over the new kitchen and bathroom. The second level continues to the right where a balcony dramatically overlooks the studio space, its floor an open steel mesh that allows light through to the area below. This balcony is populated by three lifesize papier-mâché Mexican Day of the Dead figures, dressed in conquistadores costumes, standing guard over a writing table.

The dining table is by Brian Murphy, a "signature" that most of his clients seem to end up with. A Murphy chandelier, fashioned from Tivoli lights, is suspended from the eaves. The "Dutch gable" featured on the exterior elevation houses a simple, functional kitchen finished in checked formica.

Furnished with solid antique furniture that Hopper brought from one of his previous homes—the Mabel Dodge Luhan mansion in Taos—the apartment is also enlivened by his art collection, which includes works by Bruce Conner, Andy Warhol, Marcel Duchamp, Ron Cooper, Robert Irwin, and Laddy Dill as well as his own photographs and paintings.

••

Opposite: *Three Day of the Dead figures from Mexico, dressed as conquistadores, stand guard over a small writing table in Hopper's balcony. The glass brick shower stall is visible in the opposite corner.*

The view from the dining area includes the stairs to the balcony and bedroom. Simple wood detailing is consistent with Gehry's original architectural approach.

The shower stall projects into the living space and provides light via an exterior window—a variation on a theme developed earlier in Murphy's Dixon House.

The exterior of the Dixon Residence is camouflaged with roofing, felt-covered windows and graffiti. The entry door is in the middle (top). *Recessed behind screen walls, the glass top of the dining table is supported by three bricks on a base of concrete cylinders* (bottom).

The Dixon House

Los Angeles is famous for its brash "Hey! This is me" residences. The Dixon House is quite the opposite: a nondescript wall covered in graffiti and windows mysteriously blanked off with bituminous felt wall tiles are all that is visible from an equally unprepossessing street.

Owner Philip Dixon, a young fashion photographer, bought the bungalow and adjoining disused corner grocery as the only affordable property close to the beach. Situated in the middle of the Venice Ghetto, it was not the place to make a high-profile architectural statement. Therefore, the intent was to perpetuate the "run down" look, and leave the graffiti gangs to complete the disguise.

Brian Murphy was responsible for both the exterior and interior redesign, and he arrived at solutions which present a dramatic contrast between the two. The steel-grilled entry door opens to reveal a different world: the top-lit hallway is gleaming white; the metal-grill floor is suspended over white gravel. At the end are two doors of flush stainless steel—doors without handles, only keyholes; one leading to the studio, the other to the house.

The owner's dislike of the normal accoutrements of living—books, furniture, TV, stereo system, even magazines—caused Murphy to create an austere interior with unusual architectural features and super-cool detailing. There is a toughness about everything here: walls are blank, unpunctuated by windows or pictures. The ceiling has been removed to reveal the roof space. Steel tension wires carry the structural load from wall to wall. Skylights, baffled for security, provide a beautifully soft quality of light.

The fireplace is a stunning assemblage set into a glazed section of wall, its catalogue-order fire-unit surmounted by a slab of translucent onyx which Murphy had collected on his travels. The glazed wall is punctuated by 2-by-4s to provide security and the low Murphy coffee table echoes these materials in its wood-stud and wired-glass composition.

Other unusual features include paired In and Out doors, faced in stainless steel, which give access to the patio. The dining area, half concealed behind beams and screen walls, leads to a tiny kitchen. The glass dining table top sits on three bricks resting on concrete cylinders. The chairs are highly collectable aluminum institutional chairs from the 1940s. The kitchen is not heavily used; its owner usually eats out.

In the bedroom, a glass-brick bathtub coincides with a glass-brick exterior wall, immediately opposite the bed, allowing the tub to act as a window. The bed is a tatami platform with a smooth cement curb. The room itself consists of two smaller rooms. A "strongback" beam, needed to carry the load of the considerable ceiling area, is above the roof, with the roof beams suspended from it; the attractive butterfly profile of the ceiling is thus unimpeded. The beam continues out beyond the side walls of the house to create a flying buttress.

The yard is rendered private by its wall of pine and cedar trees—chosen for their rapid rate of growth. The deck, its shape responding to the geometry of the house, floats over a bed of gray gravel. Maintenance is low, in fact almost nonexistent: the grass is a tufted variety that never needs cutting. The yard is as serene as the house. Together they make a tranquil oasis—exactly what the owner wanted.

A view of the exterior at twilight shows the fireplace wall and exterior wood deck.

The ingenious bathing recess at one end of the bedroom serves the extra function of helping to illuminate the room.

A minimal bedroom. The tatami bed has a raised cement curb and faces the glass brick bathing recess, sharing its dimensions. A large baffled skylight settles a soft light on the space.

Opposite: *From the exterior wood deck, this simple glass brick wall surprisingly conceals the bathing recess within. Detailing everywhere is pragmatic and understated.*

The living space with its single, statutory chair. The small kitchen and dining area is to the left. The top-lit entry lobby, visible through a stainless-steel door, faces a similar door to Dixon's studio. The painting is by Pat Patterson.

Opposite: *The fireplace is a stunning assemblage set into a glazed section of wall.*

CHAPTER 3

HOLLYWOOD

Hollywood epitomizes all the mythical characteristics of Los Angeles: sun, palm trees, the graphic and unique Hockneyesque cityscape, exotic architecture and amusingly kitsch buildings and institutions. Very much the center for L.A.'s café society, Hollywood is well-furnished with stylish restaurants, art galleries and the best clothing stores in the city, all found on La Brea and Melrose Avenues and La Cienega Boulevard. Rents are not excessive, and it is centrally located. It also retains its own distinctive personality, character and sense of place, qualities lacking in much of the rest of the city.

Hollywood has long attracted a cosmopolitan coterie of artists, writers and architects. Rudolph Schindler lived and worked in his historic house on Kings Road in West Hollywood (recently funded for restoration by the City of West Hollywood) from the early 1920s until his death in 1953. Kings Road also served as home, for a while, to Theodore Dreiser and Aldous Huxley. Man Ray lived in Hollywood; Ed Ruscha and David Hockney are both long-established residents.

Topographically, Hollywood divides into two distinct areas: the Flatlands and the Hills. The former, to the south, is the less glamorous residential community which shares its territory with commercial activities. Its quiet, leafy streets are lined with *bijoux* cottages, and neat front lawns adjoin other streets occupied by the sprawling sound stages, processing labs and production offices of L.A.'s film, TV and music-recording industries.

To the west of this, and smaller in area, the newly independent city of West Hollywood is squeezed between Hollywood itself and Beverly Hills. This is the center for the furniture and interior design industries, and is dominated by

Cesar Pelli's huge Pacific Design Center, often referred to as "The Blue Whale." It is an area notable for its romantic 1920s and 1930s apartment buildings, in styles which range from French Gothic to Art Deco. (The David James Residence featured in this chapter is located in one of these.) Closer to Beverly Hills is the Decorator District where tiny 1920s cottages have been "exterior decorated" with new façades in a variety of overscaled treatments, ranging from the frou-frou to the grandiose, which mimic the more regal excesses of Beverly Hills. The Rucker House, for example, has kept the fantasy for the back of the house, in the form of a sharp-edged addition by Brian Murphy.

The Hollywood Hills begin north of Hollywood Boulevard and extend all the way up to Mulholland Drive which runs along the top. The Hills comprise a series of steep canyons and narrow, winding streets containing everything from cabins to castles. Life styles range from the idyllic—landscaped terraces of Mediterranean mansions offering serene views over the city—to the surreal: Cape Cod cottages cantilevered over chaparral-lined voids, on the slenderest of steel supports, defying both gravity and logic. The indigenous wildlife includes coyotes, deer, raccoons, hawks and hummingbirds, all contributing to an ambience akin to that of an exotic wilderness.

Also exotic is the variety of remarkable houses built earlier in the century by Frank Lloyd Wright (including his Storer House), his son Lloyd Wright, Neutra, Schindler, and later, Lautner, Gregory Ain and Harwell Harris. The lavish landscape is of palms, eucalyptus and the pencil-slim Hollywood cypress, mingling with subtropical foliage of great variety. (Photography of many of the earlier houses is now impossible

due to plant growth. Whereas original photographs show the buildings in splendid isolation, they are now more or less submerged in foliage.) Above are the still-bare hilltops, a reminder of the days before the importation of water, when Hollywood was sometimes referred to as La Nopalera–The Cactus Patch.

The three Hollywood Hills projects in this chapter–a new house, a renovation and an exotic pool–only hint at the diversity of life style in this inner-city wilderness.

Houston Residence

Screenwriter Bobby Houston lives in a simple 1950s box slung over a carport and ground floor office. This building asks to be placed on a flat, horizontal plane, but is instead at the top end of a steep street, hills rising on all sides. Brian Murphy has renovated the interior, painted the exterior steel frame a bright yellow, and provided a wood deck at the back of the house with an inset lap swimming pool. The hillside is so steep that one side of the deck is set against the slope, while the other side aligns with the upstairs living area.

Inside, Murphy has provided a renovation appropriate to a bachelor with style and taste. Houston's art collection and colorful furniture is displayed in a setting of white walls, black Astroturf carpeting and a sandblasted timber roof. The Murphy wall sconces consist of drafting triangles in an unusual homage to the design process, proof that inspiration can be found by looking no further than the drawing board.

A Murphy table, also found in several other Murphy projects, fits neatly into the dining space.

The Houston Residence is surrounded on three sides by a steep-sided canyon. Its steel-framed exterior has been brightened with yellow paint and new tilework.

Opposite: *A Murphy wall sconce.*

The Houston living room, with prints by Keith Haring, can be seen from beyond a stair landing.

Above left: *Black Astroturf carpeting, white walls and sandblasted timber beams form a crisp background for the living room. Corrugated-cardboard sculpture on fireplace is by L.A. artist Billy Lobo.*

Left: *The bright dining recess adjoins the kitchen. Murphy designed the dining table and chose office chairs for seating. The small table in corrugated cardboard is by Billy Lobo.*

With murals by Malibu graffiti artists Eaz and Kiz,
Houston's downstairs office is ready for business.

Overleaf: *The living room has colorful Magistretti chairs*
and a 1950s Diamond chair by Bertoia; the large wallpiece
is the work of Robert Longo.

The Houston kitchen with its new skylight and floor light.

A duplicate of a table Murphy earlier made for himself, its construction consists of 2-by-4s with a wired glass top, decorated with colored resin corners. Although its ultra-cheap construction was dictated by economic constraints, since its origination at least three of his clients have been attracted by its chic appearance and have demanded duplicates.

The Houston kitchen is illuminated from top and bottom by square glass panels: a skylight above; a floor light below which projects light up from the bathroom spotlights underneath.

Murphy has covered the yard, which sloped steeply from the property-line fence down to the house, with a new wood deck and pool. Rather than recessing the pool into the ground, Murphy has raised it up from grade to the level of the upper living floor. It is a narrow pool, designed for swimming laps (as evidenced by the overscaled timing clock at one end).

Walking out from the living room onto the deck, which is designed as a series of interwoven catwalks floating over a void, one becomes aware of the chaparral-covered hills encircling the house, and of an almost constant breeze rising from the canyon, rippling the pool's surface. "The most poetic thing about the pool," Houston says, "is that when I'm swimming my favorite stroke, which is appropriately the butterfly, it feels as if I'm flying in space."

Murphy designed the new deck as a series of interwoven catwalks. The pool, intended for swimming laps, has an overscaled timing clock at one end. Both pool and deck are raised above grade.

Opposite: The new back elevation of the Rucker House reveals many of Murphy's characteristic "White Trash Modern" details. Note the 1–5–10–15 glazing sequence of the doors (top). The new bedroom reveals the flip side of the faceted exterior-wall treatment (bottom).

The Rucker House

Emerging from the rear of a West Hollywood bungalow belonging to screenwriter Alan Rucker and his wife Anne-Marie is an early extension designed by Brian Murphy. In a neighborhood where small houses are threatened by new condominium development, this one at least looks as if it is ready to bite back.

In a style described by the architect as "White Trash Modern," the extension provides extra living space and a bedroom along with a small conservatory covered in corrugated fiberglass. Its architectural features include a jagged profile in striped asbestos roofing felt on one side, and a row of picked-from-the-catalog doors in a 1–5–10–15 glazing pattern. These doors open onto a wood deck with inset jacuzzi overlooking a miniature tropical landscape, thereby creating a writer's retreat in the midst of a busy city.

The Jorgenson House

The Jorgenson House (1983) is built on a narrow south-facing spur high above Sunset Boulevard in West Hollywood. The spur ends in a virtual cliff, the land dropping away steeply on three sides affording dramatic views through 180 degrees, from the Griffith Observatory in the east to Century City and the coast in the west and, on a clear day, to Catalina Island.

Architect Fred Fisher conceived the house as a ruin, placing building fragments in the landscape around the house, this terrain having been left in its natural desert state: in the spring, wild grasses and flowers cover the slopes, gradually dying off

with summer. The house is intended to be a guest house and studio for owner Kim Jorgenson, who is a movie writer. It is located to the rear of a 1950s house, and is approached by descending a steep pathway via an intermediate terrace.

The main floor is a single shedlike space, its fireplace nestled in the far corner between planes of glass and a small balcony. Light streams in from various windows and skylights to illuminate the rich wood beams and graphic wall treatments. A variety of concrete blocks – some colored, some split-faced to reveal a rough texture, others displaying a special glazed finish – are distributed about the wall surfaces to give a suggestion of strata and pattern to the walls, both inside and out.

At the rear of the space, away from the southern precipice, the floor is carpeted, delineating the concrete subfloor and solid ground below. The front part of the floor is hardwood, below which is the bedroom and bath. Attractive columns of galvanized steel prove to be standard drainage culvert tubes, filled with concrete and steel reinforcement for strength. They have been used ingeniously as structural columns on both floors. In fact, the aesthetic throughout this project is one in which industrial elements are combined subtly with high-quality floor surfaces and carefully modulated color. The effect is graphic and attractive.

The bedroom and bath open onto this patio surrounded by a narrow promontory which ends in a cliff. Throughout the house, Fisher has made much decorative use of concrete block in various finishes.

Opposite: *The lofty living space in the Jorgenson House enjoys spectacular views of the city and the Sunset Strip, with doors on the left providing access to the sights via a small balcony. The column is a galvanized drainage culvert filled with reinforced concrete. Garouste and Bonetti designed the "Barbarian" chair.*

130

The living room is entered through a large entry door at left. The column is a galvanized drainage culvert.

Above left: *A door leads out to a small patio. To the right is the bathroom.*

Left: *In the bathroom, Fisher has paired the decorative concrete blocks with glass bricks.*

The dramatic view from the patio, downtown skyscrapers in the background. The columns in the foreground suggest a "ruin," in the midst of which rises the new house.

The Comegys Pool

The influence of Mexico, only 150 miles from Los Angeles, is widely felt in the city, which once was Mexican territory after all (Mexico ceded California to the United States in 1848). Such influence is reflected in the exotic swimming pool and terracing that designer Luis Ortega built into the hillside at the rear of lawyer/activist Duke Comegys's Outpost Canyon Residence in 1982.

This pool (*opposite*) illustrates Cuban-born Ortega's love of tropical colors and forms, and particularly the work of Luis Barragan who often enhanced his customary use of simple rectilinear forms and strong colors with the reflective presence of water.

David James Interior

Interior designer David James inherited a classic Hollywood-Gothic apartment on Fountain Avenue in West Hollywood, an area rich in such pretty apartment buildings from the 1920s in a variety of Medieval and Renaissance styles. (Actress Bette Davis lives in a French chateau just around the corner. There may very well be as many "chateaux" in this part of L.A. as there are in the Loire Valley.)

Working with the romantic architectural elements, and respecting their intrinsic qualities, James has designed a stylish apartment appropriate to its setting in the midst of a new cosmopolitan Hollywood; one which reinvents the glamorous Hollywood interiors of the 1930s and 1940s.

Subtle colors and finishes enrich the 1920s Hollywood Gothic apartment of designer David James.

James designed the steel headboard of the stylishly disheveled bed. The window has a view over Hollywood rooftops. The side table is by Eileen Gray, the painting by Bonnie Born.

Above left: *The bedroom. A balcony outside overlooks the double-height living space. The painting in the passage is by Mary Woronov.*

Opposite: *A dining table and chairs by James can be glimpsed beyond the pale* eau de Nil *archway supporting the stairs.*

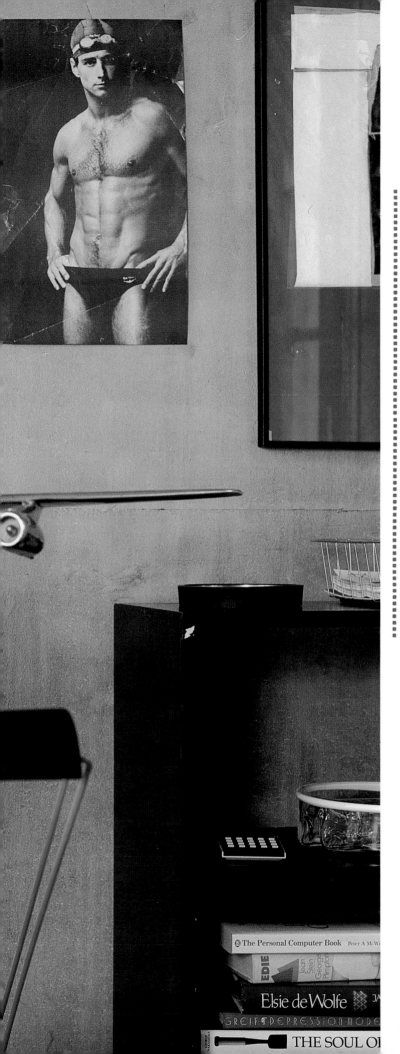

Above and opposite: *James washed the existing white-painted walls with black watercolor, allowing it to trickle into the cracks to produce an interesting patina. The painting is by Mary Woronov; the Corvette muffler is a decorative* objet trouvé *added by James.*

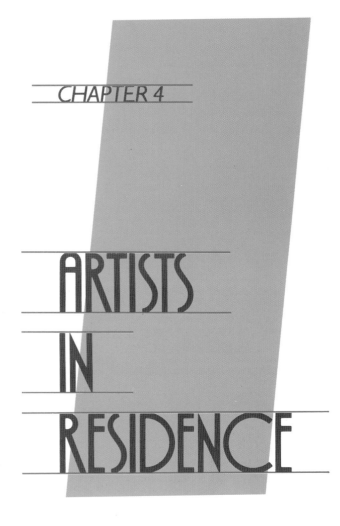

CHAPTER 4

ARTISTS IN RESIDENCE

The inclination of artists to modify their domestic environments as extensions of their work is a natural one, but few actually do so. Many artists instead live in Bohemian clutter, or they hire an architect and become chic and ordered. In Los Angeles, a few artists have chosen to develop their homes in ways which relate to their own creative work and, in the process, have shared some of the influences that have shaped the new L.A. architecture.

To live in Los Angeles is to be aware of a set of cultural influences quite unlike those of the East Coast or, for that matter, anywhere else in the country. These influences include the "American West" (both real and mythical), a surrounding landscape of deserts and mountain ranges which physically separates Southern California from the rest of the country, a brilliant and luminous quality of light and an indigenous Mexican, Spanish and Native American heritage. Geographically isolated from the East Coast and its cultural parent, Europe, L.A. instead turns to the Pacific Rim cultures to the west and south, particularly those of Japan and Mexico. Finally, there is the graphic look of L.A. itself. A cityscape like no other, it was first eulogized by Reyner Banham in his 1971 book *Los Angeles: The Architecture of the Four Ecologies,* and by David Hockney in his 1960s paintings.

L.A. artists have responded to these influences in various ways. Just as architects Frank Gehry and Morphosis have mined the industrial and back-alley streetscapes of Los Angeles for architectural references, so artists have mined the city. Jim Ganzer, for example, has used the fruit stems of that durable L.A. icon,

the palm tree – harvested from the sidewalks around his Venice studio after storms – in the construction of his Ganzer Stands.

The artists discussed in this chapter have created interiors that reflect both these L.A. influences and the diversity of vision that is possible in a city as heterogeneous as Los Angeles.

April Greiman and Peter Shire both use the vivid colors of Mexican carnivals in their work. Annie Kelly works with a quieter, though still "Mexican," palette that reflects the colors of the walls and buildings in the old colonial cities. Another suggestion of Mexico – that of the minimalist architecture of Luis Barragan – is found in the studio home of Charles and Katie Arnoldi.

The desert was evoked in Greiman's earlier apartment "landscape," as it also is by Paul Fortune's cactus lamp. In Ros Cross and Mick Haggerty's home, 1960s furniture, suggestions of Japan and decorative references to the American West coexist within the confines of a typical 1950s house.

By contrast, Lisa Lombardi and Mo McDermott occupy a tiny, charming cottage resembling an English Bloomsbury Group atelier unexpectedly transposed to a Los Angeles hillside.

In an earlier apartment, Greiman covered an ugly carpet with raw canvas, simulating a "desert" environment.

April Greiman

Graphic designer April Greiman moved to Los Angeles in 1975 and her work became synonymous with the graphics movement of the late 1970s known as the L.A. New Wave. Her innovative contributions to graphic design include the utilization of type itself as a design element. She often suggests the presence of space and

Opposite and page 139: *April Greiman's laboratories for her graphic-design experiments. Furniture and lamp fixtures are incorporated into an abstract three-dimensional artwork.*

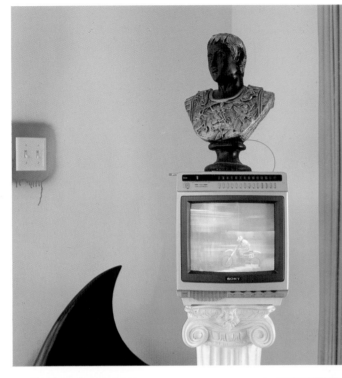

The Cross-Haggerty Residence. An eclectic corner of the living room (top). The dining area with 1960s dining furniture and a painting by Ros Cross (bottom).

perspective by varying the scale of the type across the image surface and then punctuates this with Kandinskyesque dots and squiggles. Grid motifs, to give an effect of layering, were adopted for her work – a device which has become widely used by designers everywhere, and even by architects (Eric Moss used a grid pattern on the façade of his 708 House in 1979, for example). Greiman's use of vivid Mexican-inspired color also distinguishes her palette from that of her colleagues in London and New York.

In the late 1970s, Greiman lived in the Los Altos apartment building on Wilshire Boulevard which was built in the 1920s by William Randolph Hearst, and which has been home to a number of writers and artists. Here raw canvas was tacked over an ugly carpet inherited from the previous tenant – creating an echo of the nearby desert landscape.

In 1981, Greiman moved into her house in the Larchmont District near Hollywood, where she has used her living room as a laboratory for graphic design, creating a three-dimensional environment in which abstract colors and shapes prevail over the more familiar profiles of furniture and household objects.

The Cross/Haggerty House

Artist Ros Cross and Mick Haggerty, a rock-video director whose work as an illustrator in the 1970s placed him at the forefront of the L.A. New Wave graphics movement, bought their house in 1978. Newly graduated from art school, they had arrived from London four years earlier, intending only to visit. Instead, they were immediately attracted by the 1950s architecture of Los

142

Angeles, and by the availability of 1950s furniture and automobiles—one of their first purchases was a 1959 Cadillac—and they decided to stay.

Searching for a house which "looked like a motel," they found just the thing in Beachwood Canyon. By stripping it of inappropriate wood shingles and extraneous interior walls, they were able to restore the house to its basic simplicity, and also to reveal the attractive view from its full-depth windows of the adjacent valley. Cross planted the surrounding landscape with hundreds of desert plants and created a raked Japanese garden at one end which she fenced in to exclude deer and other wild animals.

The interior of the house closely reflects Cross and Haggerty's artistic and intellectual preoccupations. The basically white living room is always filled with light and acts as a background for the painted areas added by Cross: the colors, pale and muted elsewhere, become rich and deep around the entrance, and a suggestion of pattern can be seen running up the window mullions. Cross has developed this area as a natural extension of her art and her fabric designs.

The kitchen had previously been an enclosed room, but in the course of remodeling it was opened out, and a breakfast counter was installed. The bedroom was also remodeled with the addition of an angled skylight as well as a narrow horizontal window at ground level that permits the observation of raccoons and other animals from the room (with the help of exterior lighting).

By the time the living room was painted in 1982, Cross and Haggerty's enthusiasm for the 1950s had become tempered with familiarity. Their environment now reflected new influences: the 1960s, Japan, and motifs from the desert and the American West.

Colors and applied paintwork are intensified around the entry (top). *The bedspread and painting are by Cross; the couple collaborated on the angled skylight* (bottom).

The living room combines 1950s and 1960s furniture with applied paintwork by Cross.

Opposite: *Wall decorations reflect the owners' affinity for the deserts which surround Los Angeles.*

In the Lombardi/McDermott House an eighteenth-century English chair by Linnet coexists with Anna Silver's giant teapot and Mo McDermott's "Temple of Apollo" wall light.

....

Opposite: A colorful mélange of painted surfaces reminiscent of Bloomsbury. McDermott painted the fireplace and mirror frame.

....

Below: The yellow dining room is further brightened with fresh flowers from the garden. The "Pompeiian Temple" light (on shelf) is by McDermott.

148

Lombardi and McDermott

Artists Lisa Lombardi and Mo McDermott live in a pretty 1920s cottage adjoining Elysian Park. Their garden is lined with columbine, foxgloves, roses, delphiniums and other flowers more usually seen in English country gardens, and the downtown L.A. skyscrapers seem to loom over the cottage roof.

Lombardi—who is from San Francisco—creates sculpture and painted furniture which resembles plant forms and overscaled household objects. Her vegetable table and chairs can be seen to spectacular effect in the kitchen of the Brian Murphy Santa Monica House. McDermott, an Englishman, first became known in the 1960s for his painted cut-out palm trees, which were used as free-standing screens and room dividers. He has recently been working on a series of wall-pieces, sometimes incorporating light fixtures, based on Classical allegories. Together, they have fashioned the inside of their home into a cosy, updated version of the 1930s English Bloomsbury Group salons: fresh, hand-painted surfaces and antiques mingle together in a relaxed, lived-in manner unique to English interiors.

Although avoiding the obvious Southern California influences on their life styles, Lombardi and McDermott continue the tradition of Angelino eclecticism, which has led to a proliferation of houses influenced by styles from all over the world. Their English cottage is just another way to be at home in Los Angeles.

Above left: *The dining table and cactus light (on shelf) are by Lombardi.*

Left: *McDermott painted the cabinet in the study; the side table is by Lombardi.*

The Fortune Experiments

In designing the Earthquake Bedroom, English designer Paul Fortune has perpetuated the British tradition of making jokes about adversity. Not that he is unaware of the seriousness of the earthquake threat: he personally stores eight gallons of bottled water in deference to earthquake preparedness; indeed, his inspiration for the project arose from experiencing a tremor while visiting another client. Fortune came to live in Los Angeles after having studied art in England, and he has worked on a wide range of interiors projects as well as having designed furniture and lamps.

The bedroom belongs to Graham Henman, a director of TV commercials, and it is situated in his spectacular 1950s Hollywood Hills house, built by one of the original designers of Disneyland. The room has dramatic views across the San Fernando Valley—toward the infamous San Andreas Fault. The bed is more comfortable than it looks: the rocks are foam rubber and make very comfortable cushions. The spread is stenciled with a column-fragment pattern that recalls Roman ruins. Raised on a platform of malachite-patterned Formica, the bed is eerily illuminated by twisted rods of white neon.

In 1980, Fortune designed a cactus lamp (seen here in Fortune's own bedroom in his Laurel Canyon home) that was intended for limited production. This piece is illuminated by light projected up its acrylic "stem" by a lamp hidden in the base. It sits on a canvas, hand-painted, faux-cowskin rug, another design which illustrates his continued interest in themes derived from Los Angeles and the American West.

Overleaf: *For Graham Henman, Paul Fortune designed the Earthquake Bed with its foam-rubber "rocks"; bedspread is stenciled with tumbling column fragments, and illumination is from twisted neon rods.*

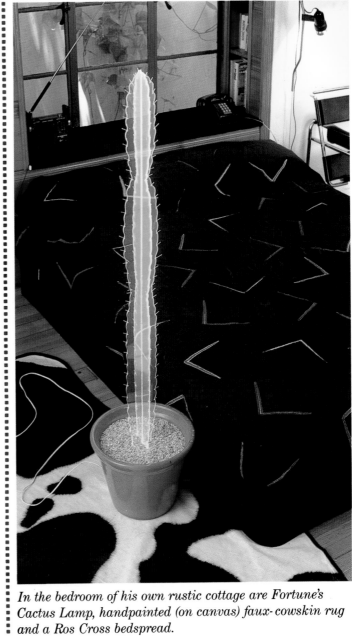

In the bedroom of his own rustic cottage are Fortune's Cactus Lamp, handpainted (on canvas) faux-cowskin rug and a Ros Cross bedspread.

A roof patio has a verandah designed by Batey and Mack. The bench is by the author.

Opposite: *A cactus garden, loquat tree and single Hollywood cypress frame the simple 1920s Spanish-style house. Yellow California poppies and red Kalanchoe add color.*

The Kelly/Street-Porter House

Annie Kelly is an Australian-born artist who concentrates on paintings and hinged screens. Her Hollywood Hills home is an unpretentious 1920s Spanish-style house which has been gradually restored to reveal its past. Kelly's attraction to Mexican interiors – in particular to the house of artist Frida Kahlo, and the interiors of the old California missions – has led in particular to a distinctive use of color, murals and friezes.

The house's exterior remains unchanged, except that architects Batey and Mack (now Mack, Architects, of San Francisco) added a covered veranda to its roof terrace in an appropriately Southwestern vernacular, but which also resembles verandas found around her family home in Australia.

Kelly's constant work on the interior of the house has led to frequent changes and reorganizations. The 1950s furniture from previous houses has been supplanted by an eclectic mix of Mexican pieces, art furniture by friends such as Phil Garner and Jim Ganzer, as well as a variety of other items picked up along the way. It has all been acquired piece by piece. As a result, each element is unusual, one way or another, and so provides continuing interest. Even kitchen appliances have been chosen carefully for their design, especially since the kitchen is visible as soon as one enters the sitting room.

The house has been renovated by using paint rather than by making structural alterations. Working with color, Kelly has succeeded in changing the apparent shape of a space. The kitchen, for example, is at the end of the living area, and its cool, receding blue makes the space appear to be longer. Upstairs, a stronger blue

"TV" chair and "Globe" lamp by Phil Garner. The chair has the added amenity of original built-in radiogram and stereo speakers.

••

Above right: The author reupholstered the 1950s couch in pale blue leather and cowhide. In front of this is a glass-topped coffee table of crossed gilded spears. The blue-and-pink frieze is by Kelly.

••

Right: Kelly's studio, with concrete floor tiles. Kelly screen is at right, and a painted wooden box, also by Kelly, sits on an equipal table from Mexico.

Opposite: Kelly painted the upper walls and ceiling of the study blue to give the illusion of greater height. Painted rug is also by Kelly.

has been used on the ceiling and upper walls of the study to create the perception of greater ceiling height.

Recently she redesigned a forgotten corner of the house as a studio, carefully approximating the house's original windows and doors (which are still being manufactured), and using cool, concrete floor tiles.

Kelly has been working on her house for over five years, using it as a laboratory to develop ideas for her screens and other art projects. This has led to an interest in interior design as an intuitive process by which the building's Spanish, Hollywood and Southwestern roots have been revealed and revitalized. She never expects—or intends—to "finish" the house, but if she ever does it will be time to move on. In that case, she hopes that her next house will be, by contrast, a futuristic "dream house" which she can fill with 1960s amoebic furniture.

Opposite: *The view into the bedroom from the roof patio. The* Flying Scarab *is by Andrew Logan, the frieze by Kelly.*

Below: *Kelly's dressing table is covered with an antique tablecloth. Jewelry includes mirrored pieces by Andrew Logan and others by Hilary Beane.*

Painted kitchen floor by Kelly. Floating on the floor behind the counter is a 1950s English cocktail cabinet.

Opposite: *The sitting room with its Garouste and Bonetti chair in painted metal, American 1940s clock and lamp, and frieze by Kelly.*

Poster by Zandra Rhodes (photo by Grant Mudford) with Kelly as model, is placed over a 1950s bureau (top). Phil Garner's "Masculini" cabinet lends a sartorial touch to the study (bottom).

Opposite: *Chintz draperies soften the dining room. The 1940s institutional chairs are made of aluminum.*

In the dining room, Shire's "Pegasus" lamp of anodized aluminum stands on a dais next to the chair from Oedipus Rex.

The Shire House

Peter Shire first made his name as a ceramic artist with his vividly colored New Wave cartoon teapots. Since 1981, he has been spending an increasing amount of time on larger-scale metal constructions and on furniture designs, which have been widely exhibited in America and also through the Italian group Memphis.

Influenced by the street colors of Mexico, and even of Echo Park, Shire's ceramics and constructions have an exuberant graphic quality. The constructions, usually of aluminum, are often anodized with exotic candy-flaked finishes hitherto seen only on California custom-cars, reminding Shire of "all the hot-rods I have never owned."

His studio is close to his home in Echo Park and is a local landmark. The brightly colored façade is sandwiched between its immediate neighbors—one covered in graffiti; the other bearing a mural depicting Aztec heroes. The neighborhood is a Mexican barrio, and the street is a narrow and winding ravine between steep hillsides, on top of which perches his spectacular new house, resembling a giant Shire teapot. This house, shared with his wife Donna and their daughter Ava, offers views of the San Bernadino Mountains to the north and the nearby downtown skyscrapers to the south. It is basically a simple tract-style bungalow that is set on a steep slope, permitting a lower floor, hidden from the street, to open out onto the garden below.

Following its metamorphosis, the house is every inch a Shire product. Undulating aluminum columns resembling giant flowers were rescued from the discotheques Shire created for the 1984 Olympics to stand on either side of the entry porch. Painted blue, yellow and red to distinguish it from the pink, fuchsia and turquoise of the house itself, this porch is capped by a green fiberglass roof. The basic functions of a porch—to welcome and shelter visitors, and to provide a pleasant moment of anticipation before entering the house—are well fulfilled here, and this is indicative of the warm, happy vision which marks all of Shire's work.

The interior of the house is small in scale, but it certainly is no disappointment. The living room is still incomplete but, in the meantime, the fireplace has been modified with columns and a concealed light has been recessed into the mantel to backlight the ceramics on display. The furniture is rotated: more permanent pieces disappear for exhibitions, or are sold, and new pieces take their place. The imposing armchair was designed for a production of *Oedipus Rex* at the Hollywood Bowl. The cabinet in the dining room is Shire's first production piece, made in 1981.

The kitchen is finished in ColorCore® Formica, allowing Shire to explore the sculptural possibilities of kitchen cabinets. He inserted a porthole in the pantry door, placing a miniature nautical tableau—which is backlit—behind it. The bathroom is a tile tour de force, each piece purposely made for the space and fired in the artist's own studio kiln.

To compensate for the miniature scale of the house, Shire's strategy has been to concentrate his efforts on the kitchen and bathroom. By giving the smallest (and most heavily trafficked) rooms the greatest intensity of surface, a feeling of luxury has been introduced which pervades the rest of the house.

Above right: *A Shire ceramic sits on his glass-topped dining table; the kitchen is in the background.*

••

Right: *The tiny Shire bathroom—a tile tour-de-force.*

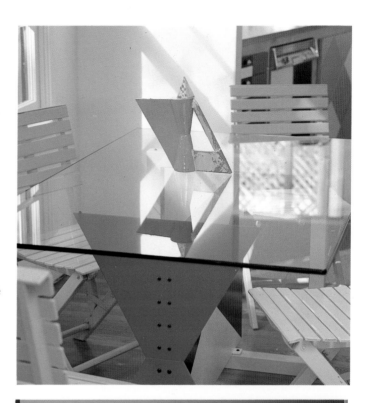

Shire spray painted this old patio chair which now sits on the small living room balcony.

Opposite: *With its undulating columns left over from the discotheques he designed for the 1984 Olympics, the residence resembles a giant Shire teapot.*

Above and opposite: *The kitchen cabinets display Shire's ceramics and kitchenware. The pantry door has an inset porthole.*

Above right: *A detail of the kitchen cabinets showing Formica-finished drawers with sculptural handles.*

Right: *Shire tiled the guest-bathroom floor in a colorful mosaic pattern.*

168

Shire welcomes visitors with a vividly colored front porch. The canopy roofing is translucent fiberglass.

The tiles were custom-made for this small, ordinary room, fired in Shire's ceramics studio, and here transformed into a work of art.

Right: *Shire custom painted cast-metal patio lights and used them as light fixtures for the corridor ceiling.*

Shire made a three-dimensional nautical tableau which can be glimpsed through the pantry door porthole. It is top-lit and built into the back of the door.

Opposite: *The fireplace has been customized with added columns and a concealed light recessed into its mantel to backlight the ceramics on display. To the left is Shire's "Obelisque" cabinet.*

The Arnoldi House

Artist Charles Arnoldi and his wife Katie have been living in a converted cottage while their new Malibu house is being completed. The cottage is part of a complex—bought by a group of Venice artists—within which existing industrial buildings were converted into studios, and a group of cottages was turned into residences and additional workspaces. Situated in the Venice Ghetto, this complex is around the corner from the Indiana Avenue studios by Frank Gehry.

The cottage is set alongside a landscaped lap pool. The small patio beside the pool creates a division between the communal and the more private areas; it leads into a living room and the bathroom which, though simple, is an elegant space with a central bathtub set in front of a cement wall, behind which are showers and a glazed courtyard.

In its use of color and the simplicity of its flat, unadorned wall surfaces, the Arnoldi House echoes the work of architect Luis Barragan.

Fronted by a lap pool, a small patio has been inset into a pale stuccoed wall. The yellow plastic discs disperse waves.

Opposite: *The new bathroom has minimal detailing with cement and tiled surfaces. Beyond is a shower and dressing area.*

CHAPTER 5

ALONG THE BEACHES

To the west and to the south, Los Angeles is edged by the Pacific Ocean—a shoreline of over seventy miles, most of which is sandy beach that is accessible to the public. From Malibu in the north to Newport Beach in the south (the venue of Schindler's historic Lovell Beach House), down to the Mexican border, the life style immortalized by the Beach Boys may be enjoyed. Unfortunately, with real estate prices reflecting the popularity of beach living, it is much easier to visit the beach than to live there.

The advantages of beach life are undeniable. The climate, tempered by onshore breezes, makes for air that is significantly cooler, not to mention less polluted, than that of Hollywood, a mere fifteen miles inland. Just having a beach to walk out on, even if it is not the prettiest beach in the world, is a considerable amenity. To look out at an unbroken horizon with nothing between yourself and Japan is a great way to clear the head and restore equanimity—the perfect antidote to urban stress.

Beach towns occur at regular intervals along the L.A. coastline. Those which most closely epitomize the legendary Beach Boys life style are located between Venice and the Palos Verdes Peninsula at the southern end of Santa Monica Bay. This string of little towns is made continuous by a fifteen-mile boardwalk and bikepath: Playa Del Rey, El Segundo, Manhattan Beach, Hermosa Beach and Redondo Beach. Venice differs from these communities due to its relatively urban character and its proximity to central L.A. with the result of huge crowds on weekends. The other beach towns are harder to reach, and there is limited parking when you do get there. On the other hand, Hermosa Beach, where the Lawrence House is located, is a quiet community which seems far removed from the hyperactivity of Venice.

The typical beach town is focused entirely on its oceanfront. The boardwalk is the artery that links one town to the next, and it also serves as a meeting place for the community. A strip of development faces the water, and behind this is found a network of streets and alleys. Density is high, oversized condominiums having been squeezed onto lots intended for the small seaside cottages which the condos have partly replaced. In these streets immediately behind the "front row," buildings appear to be jockeying for a view of the ocean like spectators at an unruly ball game. Compared to the *bijoux* scale of the original cottages, the condos—which constitute some of the world's least appealing expensive real estate—have established a new verticality (to secure the view). This and their density have had the effect of undoing much of the environmental attractiveness living at the beach otherwise entails.

This problem is of little concern to the residents however. Life appears to be leisurely and pleasant. Dedicated as they are to physical fitness, that enduring 1980s fad, residents habitually dress in exercise clothes as if they had just stepped out of the gym. As a nod to a more traditional form of exercise, they usually have a surfboard propped up beside the front door.

Of the four houses in this chapter, three are in Venice; the other is in Hermosa Beach. All share similar environmental characteristics: neighboring condos, tiny alley-size streets, and a need for verticality to compete with neighbors for view and light. Each house is squeezed onto a narrow, undersized lot with street access at both ends, and is hemmed in by adjacent buildings. Three of the houses have ocean views; the Caplin House, however, is a little too far inland, but it is metaphorically linked to the beach by its distinctive blue, wave-shaped roof.

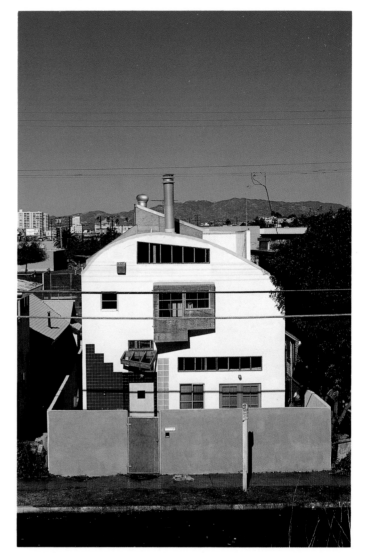

Below the wave-shaped roof profile of the Caplin House is an asymmetrical array of windows, doors and colored tile. In the background rise the Santa Monica Mountains.

176

The Caplin House

The Caplin House was the first-built project of Fred Fisher, who had earlier worked in the Gehry office (a fact that is evident in some of the house's detailing). It was commissioned by Loren Caplin, a composer, and his artist wife, Lori. Both needed studio space that is separate from the shared living areas. The property is set on a narrow, double-ended lot (with a street at each end), so the logical solution was to centrally situate the communal areas and to place the studios at either end of the house, thereby giving each its own street entrance.

Fisher designed the living room as a large, double-height space surrounded by balconies. A theatrical double staircase meets at a landing three steps up from the living room floor. After percolating through the roof structure, light filters down from various windows and skylights. The timber balustrades with their rectangular panels of chain-link fencing show an affinity with Gehry, but otherwise the design of the house explores other avenues entirely. The roof is intended to suggest the inverted hull of a boat, evoking childhood memories for Lori Caplin who grew up in a houseboat on the Seine. From the exterior, this roof resembles a giant shorebound wave.

Fisher has combined some of Gehry's approaches to detailing with a fresh, confident graphic style and a romantic use of metaphor. The result is a house that delights in its complexity while remaining well-mannered.

....

Above left: *Skylights in the bathroom provide light attractively filtered by wood slats.*

....

Left and opposite: *The lofty atriumlike living space is surrounded by balconies with chain-link balustrades.*

178

Heated by the flue of a fireplace on the floor below, the bedroom features a bed raised on a neatly articulated platform with storage below. The poster advertises the defunct magazine, Wet, produced in Venice and influential in promoting L.A. New Wave graphics in the 1970s.

Openings in the dining room provide access to the living space. The overhead balcony is edged with chain link.

Opposite: *The study opens onto stairs leading to the roof terrace. The enveloping roof form is a constant presence throughout the house.*

The Spiller Duplex

Like the Caplin House, the Spiller Duplex is in Venice, designed for film-maker Jane Spiller. It was built in 1980 by Frank Gehry, following soon after his own house conversion in Santa Monica. Gehry has squeezed a considerable amount of accommodation into the minimal 90-foot-by-30-foot lot: a rentable two-story unit complete with a tiny garden is in front, while at the rear a three-story tower, approached via a private courtyard, is built over a four-car garage. The tower evolved due to strict zoning regulations which limit the floor/site area ratio, and it combines an adequate floor area with sweeping oceanfront views from the living areas.

The tower is clad in corrugated metal but Gehry has selectively revealed the rhythm of its underlying timber-framed structure. The warmth of the wood, which has been left exposed throughout the interior, contrasts nicely with the coolness of the metal. The smooth verticality of the forms becomes fragmented at roof level, particularly above the two-story unit where skewed solar panels, skylights, a trellis and an angled bay window create a jazzy dissonance.

You enter the house through a small courtyard, planted with royal palms, then up a steep flight of steps. Outside the living area is a small patio covered by an angled trellis gradually being taken over by multicolored bougainvillaea. Inside, the interior staircase, which begins at the lower bedroom level, ascends and enfolds the living area, then continues up to a sleeping platform/guest bedroom over the kitchen. It then continues up to the roof terrace with its spectacular views over the sand and palms of Venice Beach.

Seen here from the entry courtyard planted with royal palms, the living tower's corrugated-metal sheathing accentuates its verticality.

Opposite: *Although small in plan, the living space feels lavish. Using a variety of means, Gehry has transformed a small space into one which appears much larger: the vertical timber elements above the fireplace, for example, simultaneously add depth and dramatize verticality.*

The Spillers' living space is filled with light from huge skylights overhead.

Above the living area, the stairs merge with the windows and other visible structural elements: layers of wood and metal juxtaposed in a dense collage through which light streams in a succession of changing patterns. The glazing is arranged to provide complete privacy, yet occupants can sit in the living room and watch the moon rise, following its full trajectory into the sky.

The design vocabulary Gehry used here was pioneered in his own house, but this time it was dictated by an ultra-low budget. The aim was to visually exploit the cheapest building materials – particularly the construction-grade timber which Gehry favored for its warmth and irregularity. Ignoring convention, nails, joist hangers, and metal drywall edging strips are exposed as part of the visual fabric.

Ingenious planning for a tiny lot has produced a house full of surprises, turning austerity into the considerable amenity of a rich environment of wood, white walls, space and light.

The Lawrence House

Toward the southern end of Santa Monica Bay is the quiet community of Hermosa Beach, the location for a 1983 house by Morphosis. The owners are William and Dorothy Lawrence, a retired couple who wanted a substantial house in which to live and accommodate visiting family members and friends.

A single row of houses separates the Lawrence property from the ocean so, to take advantage of the view, Morphosis planned the house upside down. Living spaces are on top and bedrooms below with a garage occupying the

Opposite: An enclosed patio can be seen through openings in the Lawrence House's galvanized rear wall. Behind this, a pitched, asphalt-shingled roof rises within the confines of the metal-clad outer envelope. The four-story height ensures a view of the ocean.

182

Morphosis designed a number of controlled vistas throughout the house. Here the kitchen is glimpsed through an opening on the opposite side of the light well.

186

ground floor. The lot is small (30-by-85 feet) which meant that four floors were necessary to yield sufficient living space.

The entry is approached via a passage midway between the front and rear of the house. Inside the glazed entry doors, Morphosis has created a semicircular lobby which projects up to the roof, acting as a light well and providing the central focus of the house: interior circulation revolves around this area at all levels. Twin stairs, necessary to meet building codes, are placed on either side of the circulation shaft, thereby providing a choice of routes and orientations as you progress up or down through the house. The principal living rooms can be glimpsed through thresholds, and they often occur at levels intermediate to the main floor, adding an interest and complexity to movement around the house. Rooms are not overly large, but of a comfortable scale, and are equipped with fireplaces.

The capacious kitchen has marble-topped counters and shares a lofty pitched roof with the extended lobby space. The adjacent dining area overlooks the living room from a higher level and the ocean beyond is glimpsed through its large metal-framed windows.

The house is clad in galvanized metal which is accumulating a rich erosive patina from the sea air. With its finely etched seams forming a raised grid over rectangular surfaces, the house presents an austere and elegant face to the street and to the sea.

Preceding pages: *The entry doors are set into a wall of glass brick. Within, the lobby is at the foot of a semicircular space which continues up to the roof* (left). *Interior circulation revolves around the semicircular lobby at each level. From this upper-level balcony, the bathroom can be seen through an opening above* (right).

Above and above left: *The austere façade is clad in galvanized metal with delicately detailed seams; its patina is acquired from the erosive sea air.*

Overleaf: *The master bathroom seen from an adjacent dressing area* (top left). *The kitchen is open to the pitched roof above, a space it shares with the vertically extended vestibule. The counters are topped with marble* (bottom left). *The living room with its granite fireplace* (right).

The Norton House

Built in 1983, the Norton House is a relatively recent project by Frank Gehry, and is located on a quiet stretch of the Venice boardwalk, with uninterrupted views of sand, palms and surf. The house is fringed by the usual motley condos and bungalows. Its neighbor, however, is a 1920s cottage in true beachcomber tradition.

Bill and Lynn Norton, a movie director and a script supervisor respectively, wanted the house for living, working and entertaining. It needed to be open to the view, yet not exposed to the public parade.

Gehry placed the living rooms behind a large open terrace on the second floor. Below this is Lynn's ground-floor office, covered in blue tile, and at its side, steps lead up from the entry gate to the terrace. A further flight of steps can be seen in the same alignment continuing on up from the third level to the roof. This offset stair axis plays an important role in the design of the building, in which a series of discrete elements combine together to complete a total composition.

The most conspicuous of these elements is the metaphoric "lifeguard" tower. Gehry created this vertical element near the front of the house to balance its main mass of living accommodation at the back. Knowing that Norton had worked as a lifeguard while studying at UCLA, he built him a lifeguard tower of his own, which is used as his office. This surreal gesture gives the terrace the feeling of a Robert Wilson stage set. In another compositional gesture, Gehry placed a freestanding structure of logs, complete with bark, in front of the window of Lynn Norton's office to serve as a sun shield and to provide a warm contrast to the cool metal and tile surfaces.

The interiors of the house are relatively conventional in relation to the exterior brio, but they are enlivened by the attractive use of color, and are well-planned to take advantage of the view and the light.

The Norton Residence is a bold contribution to the lively tradition of seaside architecture, rich in whimsy and evocative form. Its placement next to a vintage beachcomber cottage is felicitous: the innocence and eccentricity of the latter provide the perfect foil for the wit and sophistication of the Norton Residence.

The exterior of the Norton House mingles with those of its beachcomber neighbors. Beside the blue-tiled front unit (containing Lynn Norton's office), steps lead to the second-floor balcony, behind which is the living room. Above is the master bedroom with its small balcony, corrugated-metal canopy and steps leading up to the roof.

Opposite: *A close-up of the Norton "lifeguard tower," showing the detailing of the window canopies* (top). *The master bedroom with its view of the ocean and tower beyond a small balcony* (bottom).

Wide French doors open the sitting room to the balcony. The painting, by Roberto Chavez, hangs over chairs found by the owners on a visit to the Ivory Coast.

Right: *Inset into a bay window, the fireplace in the child's room was given a bold treatment by Gehry.*

Opposite: *Reached by a short flight of steps, the "lifeguard tower" is Bill Norton's office. A Navajo rug is highlighted by the small skylight overhead.*

CHAPTER 6

WEST SIDE STORIES

Nestling in the south-facing foothills of the Santa Monica Mountains lies one of the most desirable residential areas in California. Here is the "good life"; a place where most urban problems seem remote. This is the West Side, encompassing the comfortable enclaves of Beverly Hills, Bel Air, Westwood, Brentwood, Santa Monica and Pacific Palisades.

In contrast to its present verdant aspect, which we take so much for granted, early photos of the area show barren hillsides covered with sparse vegetation, and its transformation into a present day Garden of Eden is a marvel. Water, lacking in a desert climate, is the necessary ingredient to facilitate this, and the ambitious early city fathers were able to provide it via aqueduct and long-term contract from other parts of the state. With an adequate water supply and the ubiquitous sprinkler systems in place, the once desolate landscape has blossomed with a profusion of subtropical foliage.

The southern edge of this area can be defined by Wilshire Boulevard, which runs east to the downtown area and west to the sea at Santa Monica. North of Wilshire the real estate becomes noticeably grander until the hills begin and the grid system of streets gives way to curves enforced by the hilly terrain. This happens, generally speaking, at Sunset Boulevard, which also runs east–west, not in a straight line like Wilshire, but in a serpentine fashion until it reaches the ocean just past Pacific Palisades. North of Sunset the streets become winding lanes, overshadowed by massive trees and undergrowth.

In the areas boasting large estates, such as Bel Air, houses are only infrequently glimpsed, perhaps through gaps in the foliage or imposing security gates. This is the preserve of the Hollywood star, where the "Lifestyles of the Rich and Famous" TV crews periodically penetrate to bring us the private glimpses denied to the Stars Homes Tour buses.

Immortalized in countless movies, documentaries and TV shows, Beverly Hills is too well-known to need much mention here. The realities are interwoven with the myths, and any discrepancy between fact and fiction is probably marginal.

Despite the constant flurry of real estate activity in the most conspicuous residential area between Sunset and the business district (the average length of home occupancy in this area is a mere three to four years), there is little notable architecture to show for it. Most construction revolves around "exterior decorating," a Beverly Hills ritual whereby the exterior, as well as the interior, is customarily "redone" upon change of ownership.

Westwood is an upscale entertainment center and the home of the UCLA campus. Anyone who believes the myth that L.A. lacks street life needs only to go to Westwood which on weekends–or any night for that matter–resembles a lively European city. The showcase for L.A.'s movie industry, Westwood has more first-run movie theaters per block than anyplace else in the United States.

Brentwood, further to the west, is less frenetic. Together with Pacific Palisades, it is a staid community close to the ocean, set in rustic foothills well away from the stress of urban life.

Santa Monica is the oldest community on the West Side, set on a palisade of cliffs facing the ocean and punctuated by the venerable Santa Monica Pier. Behind Palisade Park, a European-style esplanade of magnificent palms, are large hotels, a shopping mall designed by Frank Gehry, and a handsome civic center. The residential

This 1960s Beverly Hills residence is an example of "exterior decorating." Its original, and rather classic, Chinese-Modern façade–with landscaping to match–survived until 1979 when . . .

. . . architect Chris Dawson converted the same house for its new movie-star owner, giving it a Late-Modern facelift and replacing the poodle-trees with a minimal rock-and-grass landscape.

Above and opposite: *Gehry removed old walls to produce a bright open space with round timber columns, and a new skylight with an exposed attic space. The dayroom* (opposite), *with original rock wall around its perimeter, has a large divan by Binder and Steinberg.*

areas are attractive and expensive, appealing particularly to well-heeled families wishing to benefit from a superior school system as well as an environment of clean smog-free air and cool temperatures.

The projects in this chapter are linked by their genteel surroundings, from the haute suburbia of Beverly Hills to its prim versions in Pacific Palisades and Santa Monica. Wealthy and conservative, the West Side is, nonetheless, an area containing some of the most original recently built residential architecture in America, including the Gehry Residence and the Petal House.

Cheviot Hills House

In 1977, Frank Gehry remodeled a 1940s bungalow in the Cheviot Hills near Westwood for a large corporation dealing in Japanese products and, appropriately, the architecture and decor all suggest an understated Japanese ambience. The furniture, veneered with cork and Formica, was designed for the project by Saran Binder and Lenny Steinberg, who also designed the color scheme.

In this project, Gehry debuted his concept of cutting through the wall/ceiling skin to expose the structure behind, and it led to the more substantial experiments in his own house and that of Doreen Nelson. The larger opening is in the center of the opened-up living space, where a skylight was cut into the roof above, enabling light to enter the room via an edited, open-to-view attic space. The resulting interior arrangement is simple, bright and orderly, suggestive of Japanese interiors yet retaining the character of the original house, with its attractive 1940s metal-frame windows.

Opposite: *The dining table of the Nelson House (china by Roy Lichtenstein) is surrounded by sandblasted redwood laths and studs; just one section of the original plastered wall was left intact.*

Nelson House

At the same time that Gehry was working on his own house, his sister, Doreen Nelson, had acquired a 1930s Spanish-style bungalow, also in Santa Monica. Gehry was called in to renovate the kitchen/dining wing at as little cost as possible.

Using a strategy similar to the one he employed for his own house, he stripped away the old plaster to reveal the redwood laths underneath, retaining them as the finished wall surface. One section of the plaster was left in place behind the dining table as an "archaeological" reference, as well as a way of throwing a focus onto the table.

Above the dining area, a cupola was also stripped down to the bare wood. New clerestory lights were introduced, and light bulbs were placed above the wood causing light to filter through and to highlight the natural redwood surfaces. All the wood was sandblasted and, being redwood, it has a unique warmth and richness of surface.

Redwood, a cheap building material in the 1930s, today is a luxury with its use limited to expensive finishes. By revealing the wood already there, Gehry was able to give his sister a luxurious kitchen within her budget constraints.

The 708 House

The 708 House—the home of architect Eric Moss and his family—was built in 1979 as an addition to a small ranch-meets-modern style 1949 bungalow by James Caughey. The addition, built over a garage, provides a master bedroom and bath

Street elevation showing two sides of the 708 House.

The Moss children demonstrate a gangplank which can be lowered from the bedroom to the flat roof of the original house. To the right is the top-lit staircase.

••

Opposite: *The new master bedroom with staircase. Between the windows, gangplank can be seen in closed position* (top). *The reverse side of the false gable, its presence emphasized by the bright polka-dot design* (bottom).

linked to the existing house by a new glass-roofed stair.

The forerunner of the more complex Petal House, this house is located on a quiet suburban street in conservative Pacific Palisades (once the home of Ronald and Nancy Reagan). In reality, this is a simple box made complex with decorative elements. For instance, Moss has collaged the façade with real elements such as windows, chimney and decorative surface treatments (giant numerals, a skewed grid pattern, tiled strip), as well as phony elements (false gable and flying buttress), all intricately combined to produce a startling and complex design. The street number is displayed in billboard size – one numeral on each of the three façades that are visible from the street. This exercise in supergraphics clearly goes beyond the simple communication of the number for the pizza man; it demands that you see all three façades to obtain a complete reading.

The fake gable suggests a conventional roof profile in a stylized cardboard-cut-out elevation that incorporates the cartoonlike (but real) chimney. The reverse face of the gable draws attention to its fakeness by its bright, tasteful polka-dot pattern. The tiny bathroom and dressing area windows are incorporated into the giant numerals, and the whole package is held together by a skewed grid (a motif which emerged from the L.A. New Wave graphics movement of the mid-1970s).

The overall composition has the look of a paper cut-out house in which all the elements have been stuck together a bit wrong, but it looks "right" just the same. However startling the 708 House may appear in its staid, suburban context, however, its playfulness and delicacy of detail are disarming, and there is none of the aggressiveness of the Gehry House in Santa Monica.

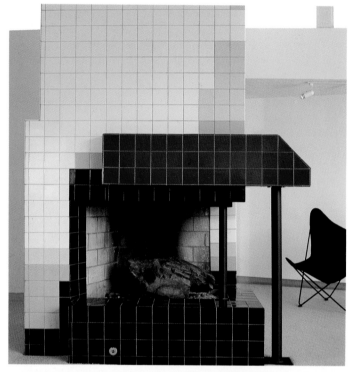

202

The Horn House

The Horn House is a 1980 remodeling by Fred Fisher. From a single-story 1950s bungalow in Bel Air, originally divided up into a number of small, dark rooms, Fisher produced a bright livable environment by removing walls to create a single space.

To break up this new large, sloping-roofed space, Fisher introduced a raised platform with tiled edge and marble steps; a freestanding fireplace of colored tile; an island counter opposite the kitchen with a playful steel column-support treatment; a stepped blue wall and sculptural bookcase. Each of these architectural "events" defines a particular activity, and together they succeed in providing cohesion to an otherwise undefined space. The window-wall at one end frames a magnificent palm, and from it a few steps lead down to a kidney-shaped pool. Altogether, this is a stylish and appropriate interior for a young bachelor about town.

Above left: *Fisher used tiled surfaces to give the freestanding fireplace a graphic treatment.*

Left: *A study area at the end of a raised platform with marble step and tiled face. The huge window, overlooking tropical foliage and a swimming pool, is a feature of the original house.*

Opposite: *Cabinets with flecked Zolatoned surfaces above the kitchen counter are supported by a metal post (left). The same counter hides a quiet office area overlooking a patio (right).*

Overleaf: *The removal of old interior walls resulted in a large bright living space with individual areas defined by a series of architectural "events." At left is a raised dining area with a table by Guy Dill.*

The old house can still be glimpsed behind the new construction. To the right is the new gallery; left, below the metal cage, is a piece by Mark di Suvero.

206

Opposite: *The stuccoed wall of the new studio and the tapered staircase leading up to a balcony. In the foreground is a Lloyd Hamrol sculpture composed of river rocks recessed into the ground.*

Brentwood House

In 1981, architects Elyse Grinstein and Jeffrey Daniels of the Grinstein/Daniels Partnership made an addition to a 1930s family house in a secluded area of Brentwood. The house's high elevation provides attractive views across Mandeville Canyon—where Thomas Mann's house can be glimpsed—to the Pacific Ocean.

The house has long served as a repository for the owners' major art collection. With the acquisition of a work by Frank Stella that was too big to fit anywhere, it seemed an opportune time to expand the wall space. Grinstein and Daniels replaced an existing sunroom at the back of the house with a new gallery. The result is a lofty, windowless space that maximizes the hanging area. A fireplace has been included as a concession to its additional function as an extra living room.

The existing terrazzo flooring of the sunroom was kept and extended over the new, larger floor area. The "footprint" of the old room's wall was picked out in a different color to serve as an "archaeological memory." Adjacent to the gallery is a small lobbylike space designed for a large Richard Serra sculpture of lead slabs resting against each other. From here, sliding doors open onto the back garden.

The rear of the house was dramatically transformed by the new construction, which consists of carefully composed, sculptural elements. The old house can still be seen behind the layers of new construction, which includes a balcony partially enclosed in wire mesh, its presence modified in a manner superficially reminiscent of the Gehry Residence. The new gallery is indicated by a large stucco form with exterior steps leading up to the balcony. These

steps are protected from the sun by a canopy of fiberglass fabric—the same type used by plant nurseries to filter sunlight—draped over the new structure.

The composition is anchored by the solidity of this stucco form. Partly concealed behind the new layering, the old house appears more veiled than caged, its matronly presence softened further by the surreal fabric which appears to have been dropped over the new roof like a discarded wrap, a romantic and mysterious gesture of which Cocteau would have approved.

Through the opening is a work in lead by Richard Serra. A hanging piece by Jackie Windsor is at right, above which hovers a dirigible by Bryan Hunt; to the left is Oldenburg's Ice Pack.

Metal steps, lit by recessed neon, lead up to the balcony which is partly sheltered by a fiberglass canopy draped over steel cables and the roof parapet.

In the gallery, a mix of family furniture is dominated by Frank Stella's huge aluminum Inaccessible Island Rail.

A large outdoor work by Charles Arnoldi occupies a quiet corner at the side of the house.

Overleaf: *From the large hammock on the balcony are seen attractive views over the Santa Monica Mountains to the ocean.*

Pages 212–213: *The new gallery room. An Ellsworth Kelly hangs to the right of the fireplace, a Donald Judd above it. On the extreme right is part of a large Rauschenberg mixed-media work.*

Grinstein and Daniels exposed the wood laths in the breakfast room for both visual effect and to improve the acoustics in a noisy family room. A Mexican chandelier hangs in front of Alan Ruppersberg's Al's Cafe, above which is another work by the artist. Jim Ganzer's "World Record" lamp—made with palm fronds and found objects—is at right.

Left: *A wood chair by artist Alex Hay stands next to a piece by Joe Goode.*

Opposite: *The dining alcove looks out onto a roof patio used for barbecues (top). In the guest bedroom, a stepped wardrobe conceals a small dressing area (bottom).*

The Koning/Eizenberg House

Hank Koning and Julie Eizenberg left their native Australia in 1979 to get masters degrees in architecture at UCLA, and they now run their busy Santa Monica–based firm, Koning/Eizenberg. The two units of their 1982 Santa Monica duplex are separated by a shared garden and a single-story unit containing studios; above this unit is a roof patio. Koning and Eizenberg live in the rear unit with their child and the front unit is rented out. Garages occupy the ground floor, the living space is on the second floor, with bedrooms on a third level.

The living room is a bright airy space heated by a freestanding wood-burning stove. An exterior-mounted sliding timber screen filters sunlight from the tall, south-facing window in the sitting area. The dining table, designed by the architects, consists of a large expanse of plywood reinforced underneath by tension wires. A breakfast area adjacent to a galley-style kitchen opens out onto the landscaped roof patio, which is often used for barbecues. The couple insisted on the careful cabinet work and high standards of finish that they were accustomed to in Australia but which are harder to achieve in L.A.

Koning and Eizenberg have here focused attention on the interior/exterior relationship. The notion of linked inside/outside spaces is something which everyone associates with Southern California, but which its architects have surprisingly ignored since the Case Study houses of the 1950s. (In Australia, its climate similar to Southern California, architects have more actively pursued an inside/outside dialogue.) Koning and

Eizenberg's handling of this relationship is immediately noticeable since the home is approached initially from the communal garden. The single story unit, which links the two houses together, meets the glazed wall of the house next to the entry door and penetrates through the glass, the roof parapet becoming the second-floor living room balustrade. When seen from the living room, looking out at the garden and its rapidly growing sycamore tree, the balustrade pushes through the glass, leading the eye out to the roof patio.

The focuses of views from the interior are primarily on these areas, stressing the existence of the garden and patio as integrated extensions of the interior living space, and reinventing a particular expression of California living.

Above left: *The living area is heated by a wood-burning stove. An exterior-mounted sliding timber screen filters direct sunlight through the south-facing window.*

Left: *Behind the large plywood dining table is a storage wall with sliding screen. To the right is the galley kitchen.*

Opposite: *The entry doors with nearby sycamore tree. The parapet of the single-story unit continues through the glass wall of the main house to become a balustrade for the second-floor living area.*

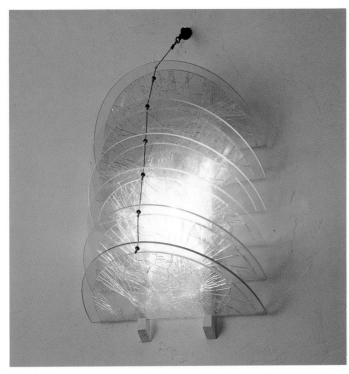

The living room sconce is shattered windshield glass sandwiched between clear-glass elements.

218

Opposite: *The staircase subtly changes color from top to bottom. The curved balustrade echoes a Deco motif set on the exterior patio. The partly seen slate shelf is a piece by Jim Ganzer.*

Santa Monica House

Although it may seem an unexpected departure for Brian Murphy after the minimalism of the Dixon Residence, his Santa Monica renovation for a movie writer and his artist wife is true to Murphy's basic tenet: to give the clients what they want (always on his terms of course).

The original house was built in 1929 in the Spanish style. The owners hired Murphy to redesign their kitchen, and then were persuaded to extend the experiments to other parts of the house. Murphy encouraged them to explore their interest in Art Deco and their attachment to things tropical and oriental. The result is an exotic, witty and unusual house which the owners like to call their "Spanish Deco Ship."

The Murphy approach throughout is to set up an effect, then to push it in another direction, all the while maintaining a visual harmony throughout. The living room, presided over by a serene Balinese garuda, hosts a mixture of elements unified by Murphy's clever use of tile. The furniture sets an impeccable Deco mood which, though nothing else in the room is suggestive of that period, manages to prevail. The ceiling is unexpectedly covered with dazzling black tiles, as is a Chinese moon-gate opening through which the sitting room can be seen. The wall sconces are made of semi-circular glass elements with fragments of windshield glass sandwiched in between. Ranged along a low window ledge are a row of L.A. designer Ron Rezek's light fixtures. The Murphy coffee table is made of two separate elements, one tiled and the other of reflective sheet-metal; the fireplace, also by Murphy, is tiled with a seductive diagonal stripe. All of this is seemingly eclectic, yet it

Above and left: *The garden, a collaboration between Murphy and landscape designer Ivy Reed, is a Tropical-Deco environment. Specially cast concrete pavers and terra cotta tiles repeat the pink-and-green grid patterns of the interior. The kitchen moon window can be seen at left. At right are French doors with a 1–5–10–15 glazing pattern.*

Opposite: *In the living room, a row of L.A. designer Ron Rezek's "Iris" lamps illuminates the coved ceiling of black tile. The pink-stained oak platform doubles as seating.*

222

becomes surprisingly homogeneous in the way it is fitted together.

The sitting room features a "tropical" bamboo couch and a carpet whose pattern recalls the tile motif on some of the exterior patios. The built-in cabinets are finished with high-gloss lacquered stripes echoing the tiled corner sconces. The French doors opening to the garden are glazed in a 1–5–10–15 sequence.

The dining room, lit by an undulating glass-block wall, and set off by a shiny blue-stained wood floor, becomes the "underwater room." When the sun shines directly through the wall, highlights from the glass blocks ripple across the floor while the blue reflects up onto the walls and ceiling. By contrast, night lighting is provided by three suspended police flashlights directing their light down through discs of shattered windshield glass.

The kitchen again features many of the tile motifs found elsewhere. Below a skylight of French glass tiles, a round window frames a view of the swimming pool fringed with banana and papyrus. This window of deeply tinted glass endows the view outside with the same brightness as that of the interior of the room, giving the illusion that it is a picture. Below the window is another fantasy: a breakfast table and chairs, shaped like vegetables, by Lisa Lombardi.

Above left and opposite: *A breakfast alcove with furniture by Lisa Lombardi. Above is a large skylight of French glass roof tiles. The moon window is tinted to render the exterior and interior brightnesses the same.*

Left: *The blue-stained oak floor of the dining room creates an underwater ambience. Night lighting is arrived at with police flashlights shining through circles of shattered windshield glass.*

In one bathroom, Murphy repeats the patterned tiling used elsewhere in the house; wall and hanging elements are corrugated fiberglass.

Above right: *In the main bathroom, the shower unit is a central glass brick cylinder with the other facilities disposed around it.*

Right: *A detail of the floor in the breakfast area showing tile patterning.*

Opposite: *The sitting room is dramatized by a lowered floor and a black-tiled ceiling. A Balinese Garuda presides serenely over Deco furniture from an Indiana movie theater and paired triangular coffee tables sheathed in tile or metal. The fireplace and keyhole doorway are also tiled.*

Masius Residence

In another Santa Monica renovation, Brian Murphy has made relatively simple improvements to a 1930s bungalow. The project for award-winning TV writer/producer John Masius was finished in 1985.

The improvements included a new swimming pool in the backyard, and some cosmetic interior embellishments, the most startling of which is a sandbagged television. Murphy also took this occasion to add a new twist to that architectural element so dear to interior decorators and post-Modernists: the Column.

Right: *This stucco-clad "twisted" column is Murphy's way of providing support for a small balcony over the carport.*

••

Opposite: *A television embedded in sandbags, a large pink saguaro cactus and a print by L.A. artist Laddie John Dill coexist in John Masius's Murphy-designed living room.*

The Weisman Addition

Gehry's addition to this 1950s house presents a discreet façade to the street. A simple rectangle of plywood with a small centrally placed window has been built over the garage.

228

Frank Gehry's addition to Marcia Weisman's Beverly Hills home was completed in 1985. The architecturally quiet 1950s single-story residence houses her distinguished art collection, including sculptures grouped around the pool in the backyard. The addition straddles the roof at one end, forming a discreet plywood-surfaced rectangle that overlooks the street.

At the back, however, the new extension takes on an imposing and dramatic presence. The interior is used as a guest house and office. A large room looks out onto the sculpture garden, the decorative view enhanced by a clever ceiling cut-back inside the window plane. The interior space is exploded at that point in anticipation of the transition between the interior and the exterior.

The exterior is clad in galvanized metal. Its wide overhanging roof, supported by angled treelike stems, extends protectively over a small balcony. A staircase curves in a helter-skelter fashion around a large ficus tree. This extension, marking a new elegance and formality in Gehry's residential work, anchors and energizes its environment.

Opposite: *Clad in galvanized metal, the addition presides dramatically over the sculpture garden. A wide overhanging roof is supported by a treelike arrangement of supports.*

The large guest room overlooks the sculpture garden and opens onto a balcony. The ceiling cut-back inside the window wall anticipates and dramatizes the spatial change between interior and exterior.

Left and opposite: A helter-skelter staircase of galvanized metal curves its way to the garden, passing in front of an imposing ficus tree. The large sculpture is a Calder stabile.

AFTERWORD

Los Angeles is forever destined to be compared to New York, and often in the manner of a child with a talented older sibling. Why does it not do everything correctly, the way its older brother did? Why does it not play by the rules? It is no secret, of course, that the child who goes his own way often turns out, upon maturity, to be the more creative, and so it is with Los Angeles. As an artistic center it is very much coming into its own in this decade, and its creative energies seem nearly limitless. The architecture that is being produced in Los Angeles is, at this moment, as fresh and important as anything being made in the United States, and it stands as a crucial complement to the often more publicized work produced on the East Coast.

One is tempted to think of it not in art historical terms but in almost emotional ones. It is surely a sensibility, not a degree of architectural knowledge, that differentiates the current generation of architects in southern California from its counterpart on the East Coast. There is less self-consciousness to the Los Angelenos, less of a sense of self-importance, less of a sense that there is a set of rules governing the making of architecture. It is right to speak of the architecture being produced here in terms of free style; true, in the hands of its best practitioners it is disciplined, but this discipline is self-imposed, not ordained from above. The Los Angeles architect sees himself as free to do what he pleases, and to make architecture that is fundamentally sensual.

This is not to say that southern California represents a dazzling, natural, unself-conscious brilliance. By no means is this the architecture of man's natural state: it is as highly studied a comment on our culture as anything produced in the East. But if the new architecture of Los Angeles is not as fully casual and laid-back as its makers might have us believe, it is nonetheless studied in a very different way from the architecture of the East. There is less of a sense of a right or a wrong way to shape form here, be it furniture, rooms or whole buildings. There is no sense that architecture needs an etiquette to govern it.

I speak of etiquette in a formal sense, not a sociological one; it has nothing whatsoever to do with being polite. It is more a matter of freedom of spirit. On the East Coast, the unspoken etiquette of architecture makes for a certain restraint, a certain blunting of emotions. In Los Angeles, the absence of this etiquette means that a matter-of-fact honesty forces its way through. It may mean that a yellow wall and a pink one are in the same room; it may mean that a roof is made to resemble the unfolding petals of a flower; it may mean that a house is designed to reveal, even after completion, the rawness of the process of construction.

Is this honesty for its own sake, an architectural equivalent of the dinner guest who speaks truth, but rudely and loudly? It might have seemed so in 1978 when Frank Gehry completed his own house in Santa Monica—the explosive deconstruction-reconstruction of an ordinary suburban Dutch Colonial house that is now so clearly an icon for a generation of younger Californians. This house at first offended its neighbors deeply and suggested that the idea of architecture as an expression of any larger contextual or communal values had no role whatsoever in the current culture of southern California. Now that the Gehry House has settled into its bourgeois quarter with a comfortable, if slightly diffident air, that conclusion seems unjust. Startling as the Gehry house was seven or eight years ago, its status as an extraordinary work of art is now beyond question. It may be the most important single-family house built in this country since Robert Venturi's 1962 house for his mother in Chestnut Hill, Philadelphia; it is surely possessed of the iconographic significance for the West Coast that the Venturi house has for the East.

The Gehry House has spurred a few nearly literal followers, such as the renovation by Elyse Grinstein and Jeffrey Daniels of a large, Spanish Colonial house in Brentwood. This is more a dutiful homage to Gehry than an original work, however, despite its fine outdoor stair; it does not push beyond Gehry so far as the exploration of materials, the relationship of new to old, and the juxtaposition of conventional, culturally accepted form and abstraction that it represents.

So one looks with more excitement to the work of architects and designers such as Eric Owen Moss, Thom Mayne and Michael Rotondi of the firm Morphosis, Frederick Fisher, Peter Shire and Brian Murphy. They—along with Gehry himself, whose recent work, if anything, confirms his continued creative energy and his position as one of the most important architects of our age—are the real focus of this book, and they seem to express best the peculiar mix of love of the past and indifference to the traditional rules of the game that marks the free-style architecture of Los Angeles.

Their work—and I group them together knowing that there is as much that separates them as unites them—is brimming over with an energy and a sensuality that seems particularly right for Los Angeles. Perhaps it is the energy that is most striking of all, the sense that these designs, be they interiors or whole buildings, are turbocharged. The drive to make architecture more sensual is one that is not southern California's alone, but has a counterpart in the post-Modern impulse of the East Coast as well; sensuality combined with such explosive energy, however, is all California's. We feel an almost electric charge in a lot of this work, from the exuberant colors of Peter Shire (or even the muted ones of Tina Beebe and Buzz Yudell) to the crisp compositions of Brian Murphy.

Murphy's work is particularly intriguing. He deals frequently in the precise arrangement of hard-edged, industrial objects, placed with as much care as the furniture in a room by Mies van der Rohe. The composition is modern, but the elements themselves are often funky, rough, even crude, and the wall surfaces and textures are often common and industrial as well. The space thus becomes a comment on ordinariness and the objects of mass-production as well as on the modernist esthetic—the juxtaposition is a conscious elevation of everyday objects to high-design status, but it is done with a certain relaxed, easy air. Murphy is clearly reveling in the funky object, not over-intellectualizing it.

Much of Murphy's work pays conscious tribute to the 1950s, a decade whose design output was wrongfully considered beneath contempt a few years ago, but which now runs the risk of being, like Art Deco, all too celebrated. And Brian Murphy is hardly alone here. The Erenberg House in particular plunders the design sensibility of that decade. To celebrate the 1950s, however, is to celebrate Los Angeles itself, for this decade seems to summarize all that was once hated about the city, and which now seems to be loved. Los Angeles in the 1950s was first coming into its own as a great city; the automobile, the freeway and the architecture of the highway strip are its symbols. These are the years that represented a kind of innocence for the larger culture of this city itself, a kind of certainty that Los Angeles really was the paradise at the end of the American road. But the 1950s also represented childhood for most of these architects. There is a certain logic, then, to the connection that has been made—for many of the free-style architects of Los Angeles, the struggle to understand the essence of Los Angeles has brought them back to their own pasts.

There is surely some of that struggle in the work of Eric Owen Moss, too, although Moss's take is very much his own. His work seems "dumb" and plain on the one hand, almost too literal in its imagery—the 708 House with its giant numbers, the Petal House with its opening leaves on the roof—yet it is also strikingly fresh and strong compositionally. This is architecture that is far more knowing and sophisticated than it at first lets on to being—in a way, Moss combines the sensibility of Frank Gehry with that of Robert Venturi.

Equally knowing, surely, is the work of Morphosis, the firm headed by the team of Thom Mayne and Michael Rotondi that has done some of the best work in Venice and, more recently, elsewhere in the Los Angeles area. The funkiness here is much more controlled, the compositions much more traditional and even classical, as in the sprightly yet taut 2–4–6–8 House or the more brooding Venice III. This time it is not Robert Venturi who is being mated to Gehry but Aldo Rossi, and the result is every bit as original as with Moss. In their Lawrence House in Hermosa Beach, Mayne and Rotondi reveal that their ability to respond to a sense of place and enhance it without in any way copying it literally is every bit as strong in a conventional, upper-middle-class beachfront community as it is in funky Venice.

This ability to understand the underlying nature of a place is, in the end, what ties together all of the diverse design work in this book. The "free style" of L.A. architecture is really not quite so free as it first appears, for it is limited and defined by Los Angeles itself, by the desire on the part of all of these designers and architects to respect what they see as the essential qualities of Los Angeles. They all see these qualities differently, of course; it almost goes without saying that Los Angeles, like all great cities, is read differently by all of us. But to interpret this city and, ultimately, to honor it is the goal of every designer and architect represented in these pages. *(P.G.)*

Index

Acknowledgments

Since arriving in Los Angeles in 1977 I have been documenting many of its unusual houses and interiors, some of which are featured in this book. This has been made possible by the patience of the architects and homeowners, and I am very grateful to them.

Annie Kelly has acted as my unofficial editor throughout the project, and the book benefits from her perception and judgment.

The majority of these photographs were initiated by me (that is, photographed on spec). Some of the others were commissioned by specific magazines, in which case I should like to thank the editors, stylists and art directors who either commissioned them or helped in their production: these include Elizabeth Sverbeyeff, Rip Georges, Lloyd Ziff, Barbara Goldstein and Steven Wagner.

House & Garden kindly allowed us to use a number of pictures for which they hold the copyright.

Thanks to Elizabeth Whiting of Elizabeth Whiting Associates in London for syndicating many of these photos in magazines around the world and for her support over the years.

I should like to thank Frank and Berta Gehry for their early assistance.

Finally, my special thanks to my editor, Roy Finamore, for doing such a wonderful job.

　　　　　　　　　　　　　　　　　–Tim Street-Porter

Design

J. C. Suarès
Diana M. Jones

Composed in Century expanded, Gill Sans bold and Univers 39 by Arkotype Inc. and Cardinal Type Service, Inc., New York, New York

Printed and bound by Toppan Printing Company, Ltd., Tokyo, Japan